A Notebook of Love

My Story on Mental Health

By

Luis Trivino

ISBN: 978-0-578-34513-0

DEDICATION

I would like to dedicate this book to my wife, if she had not presented me with her initial question. I would not have had the courage to write this. I would like to thank my family and friends for their support during the writing of this.

Contents

Chapter One

Love the Person, Accept the Illness
"The unexamined life, for a human, is not

worth living" - **Socrates**

At the time of this writing, my life and marriage are in turmoil; I have no idea what will happen from one minute to the next. She and I have been married for 14 years and together for over 15. She has borderline personality disorder (BPD), post-traumatic stress disorder (PTSD), severe anxiety, and depression. I suffer from PTSD and Bipolar Disorder. While I write this, you wonder how two people with these disorders can last this long in a relationship. For myself, it is easy, and I desire to be the man she deserves. We have been very happily married up to this point. People all around us did not suspect we both suffer from these mental illnesses; some of our closest friends consider us a power couple (a couple who has it right!). We did not keep our Mental Illnesses private. Many people in our inner circle know about our differences, disorders, and traumas. My wife and I wear them like badges of honor and hope, showing others you can do this too. We've received positive comments from family and friends, such as: "How do you guys do it?", "Wow, I never knew," "You guys just seem so perfect together," or "I wish we had what you guys have." Together we reply, "We love each other," "We understand and communicate with each other." We both wear our badges in our relationship and our mental disorders with honor.

One day, my wife asked the question after she had a very intense trauma therapy session, "Why do you love me?" Hm, I say to myself, "OH my god, this is some deep shit. I need to be careful." She asks, "Do I love her? How can I love her?" I try to analyze the situation concerning these tough questions, but I have no answer now. I said, "Why, my love? Are you ok?" She didn't answer, but the following weeks were subtle hints about her self-worth and whether she was truly worthy of love and returning it. Clearly, I can tell my wife I love her, but giving a reason and valuing her worth in a fragile mental state can be very damaging to her and our relationship.

Almost 15 years together, I learn something new about my wife every day, and I love it. What could be triggering all this? In my attempt to respond to my wife's examination of herself and life, I tried to keep it simple to reinforce it later. I said, "Baby, I love you with all of who I am, and your worth is everything our relationship and love have to offer as a couple." I said, "I know you're in a funk, but we are going to get through this together," as I grabbed her hand. I thought to myself, "This will be the most challenging thing for us both. Am I prepared? YES!" but I'm scared as hell. I sat down and tried writing my many reasons for loving her. I love your smile, quirks, company, etc., but it was too corny and not us. But I must consider this relationship is far more complicated than most while attempting to answer her question. This whole deep analysis of my marriage and an honest answer to my wife's question has me trembling. I am too scared to ask myself more profound questions because it brings out things I may not want to expose to the relationship. Is she afraid of rejection, or am I? This book turned out to be an examination of myself, and a means to convey my unconditional love, and how I relate to her. Enough of me, let's move forward with the considerations in our relationship, our disorders, and our disabilities.

According to the National Institute of Mental Health (NIMH), "Mental illnesses are common in the United States. Nearly one in five U.S. adults live with a mental illness (51.5 million in 2019). Mental illnesses include many different conditions that vary in degree of severity, ranging from mild to moderate too severe[1].

---

[1] Psychiatry.org. 2021. *What Is Mental Illness?* [online] Available at: <https://www.psychiatry.org/patients-families/what-is-mental-illness>

The statistics are astounding:

- ☐ In 2019, an estimated 51.5 million adults aged 18 or older in the United States with any mental illness (AMI). This number represented 20.6% of all U.S. adults.
- ☐ The prevalence of AMI was higher among females (24.5%) than males (16.3%).
- ☐ Young adults aged 18-25 years had the highest prevalence of AMI (29.4%) compared to adults aged 26-49 years (25.0%) and aged 50 and older (14.1%).
- ☐ The prevalence of AMI was highest among the adults reporting two or more races (31.7%), followed by White adults (22.2%).
- ☐ The prevalence of AMI was lowest among Asian adults (14.4%).

Surveys from known patients generate the statistics above. So, it is probably safe to say that there is someone with a mental disorder in every relationship in America.

I don't think anyone will know the actual number of people suffering from AMI in America. The numbers in men might be terrifying if they are semi accurately identified. We men are stuck and raised with the stigma of being tough and providing. You may even hear a father tell a son, "Be a man; there is nothing wrong with you." So, when it comes to man's self-evaluation of mental illness, we have been raised knowing we are fine (there is nothing wrong with ourselves) and be tough. Over the years, I have seen my friends apply this logic in their problem solving, and it has led many friends down some dangerous paths of self-destruction and loathing. We have all seen a "Strong Man" fall apart when his woman leaves, or the jealous rage associated when another man starts talking to his woman. The controlling man reacts to another man merely looking at his woman or looking in her direction. By grouping everything we have read above, it doesn't take a doctor to deduce the person is suffering from an AMI easily. So, what does a traditional man do to cope? Men drink, it's that simple. We have seen it in all western movies, and hear it in songs about drinking to forget a loved one. Others may use other means to deal with their internal suffering and pain, sex, drugs, any vice that helps deal with the issue because we are tough and being a man. All our friends know we are getting a divorce at this writing. That means all the Facebook messages and phone calls are coming in. I can't believe it. You both seem so happy; you are her Rock. She is your soulmate. My Native American godfather encourages me and tells me in Tewa (our native language) "Seng Wah," Be a Man (be strong), and I gratefully thank him for his advice, "Hoy."

I'm sure the story is the same for a girl, growing up playing wedding and dress up, learning they will find a man of her dreams to take care of her. Chances are it will be that same man who is raised to "Be a man." How many times have we all said, "He is just being a man, let him sow his oats," "He's strong, don't worry, he will figure it out." But, have you ever stopped, stood back, and thought to yourself, "Is there something disturbing him aside from his relationship?" How about the young hot stud muffin at the bar or the club having fun "Being a man"? He really is sowing his oats, drinking it up, then drinking again to get over the girlfriend he just lost. Is he hurting inside or suffering from the ability to properly make decisions he finds hard to make and can't face himself in the mirror, or is he "Simply being a man"? Right now, I am far from being a man or being ok. The woman I love with all my being is in a mental crisis from her mental illness. The "family," and she and I do not know the outcome.

The American Psychiatric Association (APA) defines Post Traumatic Stress Disorder as - a psychiatric disorder that may occur in people who have experienced or witnessed a traumatic event such as a natural disaster, a serious accident, a terrorist act, war/combat, or rape or who have been threatened with death, sexual violence, or serious injury[2].

The symptoms are:

1. Intrusion: Intrusive thoughts such as repeated, involuntary memories; distressing dreams; or flashbacks of the traumatic event. Flashbacks may be so vivid that people feel they are re-living the traumatic experience or seeing it before their eyes.

---

[2] Psychiatry.org. 2021. *What Is PTSD?* [online] Available at: <https://www.psychiatry.org/patients-families/ptsd/what-is-ptsd>

2. Avoidance: Avoiding reminders of the traumatic event may include avoiding people, places, activities, objects, and situations that may trigger distressing memories. People may try to avoid remembering or thinking about the traumatic event. They may resist talking about what happened or how they feel about it.

3. Alterations in cognition and mood: Inability to remember important aspects of the traumatic event, negative thoughts and feelings leading to ongoing and distorted beliefs about oneself or others (e.g., "I am bad," "No one can be trusted"); distorted thoughts about the cause or consequences of the event leading to wrongly blaming self or other; ongoing fear, horror, anger, guilt or shame; much less interest in activities previously enjoyed; feeling detached or estranged from others; or being unable to experience positive emotions (a void of happiness or satisfaction).

4. Alterations in arousal and reactivity:
   Arousal and reactive symptoms may
   include being irritable and having
   angry outbursts; behaving recklessly
   or in a self-destructive way; being
   overly watchful of one's
   surroundings in a suspecting way;
   being easily startled or having
   problems concentrating or sleeping.

The NIMH defines bipolar disorder as
follows:

Bipolar I Disorder— defined by manic
episodes that last at least seven days or by
manic symptoms that are so severe that the
person needs immediate hospital care.
Usually, depressive episodes occur as well,
typically lasting at least 2 weeks. Episodes
of depression with mixed features (having
depressive symptoms and manic symptoms
at the same time) are also possible[3].

Bipolar II Disorder— defined by a pattern of

---

[3] National Institute of Mental Health (NIMH). 2021.
Bipolar Disorder. [online] Available at:
<https://www.nimh.nih.gov/health/topics/bipolar-
disorder>

depressive episodes and hypomanic episodes, but not the full-blown manic episodes that are typical of Bipolar I Disorder.

Cyclothymic Disorder (also called Cyclothymia)— defined by periods of hypomanic symptoms as well as periods of depressive symptoms lasting for at least two years (1 year in children and adolescents). However, the symptoms do not meet the diagnostic requirements for a hypomanic episode and a depressive episode.

Symptoms of Bipolar Disorder as defined by NIMH:

People with bipolar disorder experience periods of unusually intense emotion, changes in sleep patterns and activity levels, and uncharacteristic behaviors— often without recognizing their likely harmful or undesirable effects. These distinct periods are called "mood episodes." Mood episodes are very different from the moods and behaviors that are typical for the person. During an episode, the symptoms last every day for most of the day. Episodes may also last for longer periods, such as several days or weeks.

People having a manic episode may:	People having a depressive episode may:
Feel very "up," "high," elated, or irritable or touchy	Feel very sad, "down," empty, worried, or hopeless
Feel "jumpy" or "wired"	Feel slowed down or restless
Have a decreased need for sleep	Have trouble falling asleep, wake up too early, or sleep too much
Have a loss of appetite	Experience increased appetite and weight gain
Talk very fast about a lot of different things	Talk very slowly, feel like they have nothing to say, forget a lot
Feel like their thoughts are racing	Have trouble concentrating or

	making decisions
Think they can do a lot of things at once	Feel unable to do even simple things
Do risky things that show poor judgment, such as eat and drink excessively, spend or give away a lot of money, or have reckless sex	Have little interest in almost all activities, a decreased or absent sex drive, or an inability to experience pleasure ("anhedonia")
Feel like they are unusually important, talented, or powerful	Feel hopeless or worthless, think about death or suicide

The NIMH defines Borderline Personality Disorder as follows:

Borderline personality disorder is an illness marked by an ongoing pattern of varying moods, self-image, and behavior. These symptoms often result in impulsive actions and problems in relationships. People with borderline personality disorder may

experience intense episodes of anger,
depression, and Anxiety that can last from a
few hours to days [4].

Signs and Symptoms of Borderline
Personality Disorder

People with borderline personality disorder
may experience mood swings and display
uncertainty about how they see themselves
and their role in the world. As a result, their
interests and values can change quickly.

People with borderline personality disorder
also tend to view things in extremes, such
as all good or all bad. Their opinions of
other people can also change quickly. An
individual who is seen as a friend one day
may be considered an enemy or traitor the
next. These shifting feelings can lead to
intense and unstable relationships.

Other signs or symptoms may include:

---

[4] National Institute of Mental Health (NIMH). 2021.
Borderline Personality Disorder. [online] Available at:
<https://www.nimh.nih.gov/health/topics/borderlin
e-personality-disorder>

- ⬚ Efforts to avoid real or imagined abandonment, such as rapidly initiating intimate (physical or emotional) relationships or cutting off communication with someone in anticipation of being abandoned
- ⬚ A pattern of intense and unstable relationships with family, friends, and loved ones, often swinging from extreme closeness and love (idealization) to extreme dislike or anger (devaluation)
- ⬚ Distorted and unstable self-image or sense of self
- ⬚ Impulsive and often dangerous behaviors, such as spending sprees, unsafe sex, substance abuse, reckless driving, and binge eating. Please note: If these behaviors occur primarily during a period of elevated mood or energy, they may be signs of a mood disorder—not borderline personality disorder.
- ⬚ Self-harming behavior, such as cutting
- ⬚ Recurring thoughts of suicidal behaviors or threats

- ⬚ Intense and highly changeable moods, with each episode lasting from a few hours to a few days
- ⬚ Chronic feelings of emptiness
- ⬚ Inappropriate, intense anger or problems controlling anger
- ⬚ Difficulty trusting, which is sometimes accompanied by irrational fear of other people's intentions
- ⬚ Feelings of dissociation, such as feeling cut off from oneself, seeing oneself from outside one's body, or feelings of unreality

The American Psychiatric Association defines depression as:

Depression (major depressive disorder) is a common and serious medical illness that negatively affects how you feel, the way you think, and how you act. Fortunately, it is also treatable. Depression causes feelings of sadness and/or a loss of interest in activities you once enjoyed. It can lead to a variety of emotional and physical problems and can decrease your ability to function at work and at home[5].

Depression symptoms can vary from mild to severe and can include:

- Feeling sad or having a depressed mood
- Loss of interest or pleasure in activities once enjoyed
- Changes in appetite — weight loss or gain unrelated to dieting
- Trouble sleeping or sleeping too much
- Loss of energy or increased fatigue
- Increase in purposeless physical activity (e.g., inability to sit still, pacing, handwringing) or slowed movements or speech (these actions must be severe enough to be observable by others)
- Feeling worthless or guilty
- Difficulty thinking, concentrating, or making decisions
- Thoughts of death or suicide

---

[5] Psychiatry.org. 2021. *What Is Depression?*. [online] Available at: <https://www.psychiatry.org/patients-families/depression/what-is-depression>

The American Psychological Association defines Anxiety as:

Anxiety is an emotion characterized by feelings of tension, worried thoughts, and physical changes like increased blood pressure [6]. People with anxiety disorders usually have recurring intrusive thoughts or concerns. They may avoid certain situations out of worry. They may also have physical symptoms such as sweating, trembling, dizziness, or a rapid heartbeat.

You may have skimmed through all the definitions and rhetoric of mental illness, or you may already be aware of these symptoms and behaviors. Now, you say, "WOW, those are a lot of issues and problems. I would not stick with it," or "it was doomed from the beginning." I learned to accept people for who they are, not for the many social or personal tags. In my opinion, we may ALL have AMI or mental disorders. The defining difference can be the degree of illness, and the magnitude of symptoms, triggers, and coping skills vary

---

[6] https://www.apa.org. 2021. *Anxiety*. [online] Available at: <https://www.apa.org/topics/anxiety>

from person to person. For me, it is something that Christianity preaches; God does NOT hate the sinner; he hates the sin itself. God unconditionally LOVES the sinner. So how can we hate or dislike a person for who they are or how they act, or simply how their brain functions?

The answer is, "Accept them and love them as they are. It's that simple." In my case, I love my wife unconditionally, and I am human, and that's where things can become skewed concerning love and logic. I love the quote from "O Brother, Where Art Thou?" George Clooney plays Ulysses Everett McGill, and says "Pete, it's a fool that looks for logic in the chambers of the human heart." When my wife asks me, "How can you love someone like me?" I responded, "it's simple. You are perfect as you are, disabilities included." I am not a fool in love. I don't look for logic in my heart when it comes to her, and I accept her as she is. For me, that is my unconditional love. How did we last for 15 years when the norm for BPD is seven years? Because of our disabilities combined and the risks, we may have tripled the success rate. But who knows? For us, we pride our marriage on

Chapter Two

The Family

"...the right of the parents to the management and training of the child, so long as it is itself incapable of making proper use of its body as an organism, and of its mind as an understanding." - **Immanuel Kant**

My mother was Born in Cochiti Pueblo, raised in Laguna Pueblo and her father was from San Ildefonso Pueblo. Most of the American Indian Tribes in New Mexico are of Puebloan decent; most live in northeastern Arizona and northwestern New Mexico[7] . Mom's father died when she was five years old, and her mother was of Spanish descent. One day my mother asked me if I wanted to read her journal; she explained it is therapeutic to her and she would like me to know more about her. So,

---

[7] Encyclopedia Britannica. 2021. *Pueblo Indians | History & Facts*. [online] Available at: <https://www.britannica.com/topic/Pueblo-Indians>

the following tenets: We are both committed, both dedicated, we accept each other, COMMUNICATION, and LOVE. So perhaps by now, you're wondering how we got here?

Trivino/ A Notebook of Love-My Story on Mental Health

I read it! The childhood atrocities my mother experienced were shocking. They angered me, it infuriated me, and she was standing a survivor from that past. In her journal, she describes how she was eight years old and dropped off at the Albuquerque Indian school by a total stranger in the evening. How and why she arrived is something the family and I will not share at this time. On her first morning there, she was unbathed, dirty, and the clothes she had on were old, ragged, and too small. She woke up with a bunch of girls teasing her, "oh look at her, she doesn't know how to comb her hair," "look at how dirty she is," amongst a few things. She followed all the girls as they woke and did their daily chores and personal hygiene. When all the girls finished their tasks, they ran into the kitchen. Each kid grabbed an orange and a plate with their breakfast for the day. She noticed no one ate their orange, so she followed and tagged along. Later, while all the other kids were playing outside, she was alone, sitting on a bench just looking at the orange. She didn't know what it was; she stared at it in amazement, smelled it, and "It smelled so GOOD," she states. Till her urges and impulses got the best of her. She writes how she just started to eat the orange, rind, and all. She ignored all the kids laughing at her and teasing her saying "look at her she doesn't know how to eat an orange" She thought, "IT TASTES SO GOOD!" She never knew something like that existed.

My father was born in Carlsbad, New Mexico, and is of Yaqui Indian descent from Sonora, Mexico, with a US-recognized Village in Tucson, Arizona. My dad, too, lost his father at five years old. He was a military Veteran from the Korean conflict, which affected his mental stability. Growing up, I heard many stories of my grandmother and had many experiences from her abuse. I remember I was about five years old, and my siblings and I were at my grandma's house, and we were playing outside. She made me sit on the porch alone, gave my brother, my half-siblings, and cousins ice cream except for me. I was to sit down alone because I looked too much like my dad's father. I was to sit there and not move while the rest of the kids could play. I remember one cousin saying to me, "Luis, come play with us." I responded, "I can't.

She will see." To this day, those stories bring tears to his eyes when we discuss some things in our shared memories of grandma. My mother told me my grandmother was so mad at my father for something that she beat him until he was unconscious and then stomped on his head while passed out.

At 16, my grandmother signed papers allowing my father to join the Navy. He served in Korea in the conflict and was honorably discharged years later.

My mom and Dad met in Denver, Colorado; my dad was at the famous Fort Lyon VA hospital suffering from what was called "Battle Fatigue" or "Shell Shock." Webster's Online Dictionary defines post-traumatic stress disorder occurring under wartime conditions (as combat) that cause intense stress: battle fatigue, combat fatigue[8] . My father underwent Electroshock therapy due to his rage and

---

[8] Encyclopedia Britannica. 2021. *combat fatigue | psychology*. [online] Available at: <https://www.britannica.com/science/combat-fatigue>

battle fatigue; he was divorced twice and
had four kids back in Carlsbad. I remember
him saying he could handle some of his
decisions because he did not want a
lobotomy like some other veterans. My
mother was nearby at Denver General
because she was suffering from kidney
failure due to a strep infection that settled
in her kidneys. In 1967 my mom and dad
ran into each other. It was love at first sight
for both. They have so many similarities.
Both lost their fathers at a very young age,
both were survivors of abuse and PTSD, and
both were from New Mexico and Native
American. It was an instant bond for sure.
My mom later received her kidney from a
brother and kept the same kidney for over
53 years, and had four kids.

Monsters Live 24 Hours a Day

The earliest I could form memories
and understand what I was learning is about
a little over five years old; we live in
Carlsbad, NM, with my parents, my younger
brother, sister, and me. I remember seeing
the news anchors on CBS talking about the

war in Vietnam. In the evening, news displayed the local boys killed in action as the transmission ended. I remember my dad would go bonkers when the army bugle song Taps was played in memory of the fallen. You could see the change in the color in his face turn pale then start crying or go into a fit of rage. I asked my mom what was wrong; she would rush over to us kids and comfort us and take us to a room and said he was sick in the head. She couldn't understand, but she knew something was wrong and accepted him because he accepted her with her own issues, and they both LOVE each other beyond comparison. When dad was not in a crisis or triggered by things happening in Vietnam, things were great! Dad and mom would share time and enjoy being together. They would sit and talk together while one was in the bathroom just having the most profound conversations about anything and everything. Their behavior taught me to speak with my partner, share my deepest feelings and fears, learn complex things within my relationship, and help others grow.

Dad had various jobs until he received his 100% disability rating from the Veterans Administration (VA) for Mental illness and was unemployable under VA ratings, so he couldn't get a job without losing out on his pension to raise a family of five. It took a while for Dad to get his social security disability benefit after his VA rating. Dad applied for a social security disability rating being responsible for seven kids. Money was tight for the family, affecting Dad's mood swings. One day in Carlsbad, my sister did something wrong, and my dad, being a firm believer in the belt, started to spank my sister. At one point, my sister began to scream in a pitch that placed my father into a monster; I remember him screaming, "STOP SCREAMING LIKE SOMEONE IS KILLING YOU!!" He just kept repeating it and stopped in shock, picked up my sister, hugged her and took her inside, and wept like a crying baby. My sister had some bruising and welts from the belt, but she recovered. I don't know if she remembers that, but the image on my dad's face was that of a monster! It was NOT my DAD; it was a monster. My dad loved us with a passion that all fathers do, but when he changed, he turned into a monster, the expressions on his face, the sweat coming off his brow, the heavy breathing, and then the calm down. It could be easiest described how David Banner transformed into a Hulk in the television series from the late 70s. My dad loved the show, and, in my head, he would turn into the Hulk when he was angry and violent. He, like the Hulk, led a destructive path everywhere he went in his uncontrollable rage.

My dad was always anxious, and I remember him hearing a cat walk across the carpet and waking up. So as kids, we rarely walked by dad when he was sleeping on the couch. One evening after the night of my sister's beating, I remember my dad just screaming at the top of his lungs, "THEY ARE KILLING THE BABIES! STOP KILLING THE BABIES!" my mom never woke him up. The Hulk was alive and swinging at everything the first time she woke him up. But she was there standing by to hear him and soothe him from this nightmarish flashback of Chinese and North Korean soldiers throwing babies in the air and stabbing them with bayonets as they fell. Those kinds of memories or flashbacks brought out a different type of monster, the sobbing child who tried to drink to sleep. Dad made silver jewelry and stayed up for days and nights when he was in his grove of creativity. Then when he would sleep, he would crash for days. I almost describe it as someone on meth, then sleeping when the effects wear off. The room dad used his imagination to create was called the "Indian Room." It was the Indian room because he had all products of all his makings, war bonnets, moccasins, you name it. But under his desk was a large clear bottle of his favorite drink. Sotol (Tequila) is a distillate made from a shrub, Dasylirion wheeleri, more commonly called dessert spoon. That's in contrast to Tequila and mezcal, crafted from agave[9]. The bottle to a 6-year-old was HUGE, it was underneath his silversmithing desk, and he would drink from it and play Indian music or Mexican Music. One day, my dad listened to a new album of Mexican "Corridos" (ballads). He came running out in a rage and started to SMASH the record player in a Hulk fashion, screaming "THEY ARE ALL

---

[9] 2021. *Sotol Definition & Meaning*. [online] Available at: <https://www.merriam-webster.com/dictionary/sotol>

DEAD!" repeatedly with tears running down his face. Afterward, he went to bed and sobbed himself to sleep, and mom was there picking him up emotionally and in any way she could. Dad fell into a massive depression after that. Years later, I discovered it was related to the massacre at the battle of "Pork Chop Hill." Pork Chop Hill, officially designated "Hill 255," was the site of an extended struggle along the Korean peninsula. This struggle consisted of a pair of related infantry battles that occurred during the spring and summer of 1953, and this hill was only one of several exposed hills. This line was subject to attacks from two highly trained Chinese Communist Forces divisions[10].

My dad claimed to be a Boatswain's Mate in the US NAVY. According to the Navy Cyberspace site, the Job rating was officially established in 1794. Boatswain's Mate and Gunner's Mate are the oldest, continually serving ratings in the United States Navy, and each has a rich history and

---

[10] National Veterans Memorial and Museum. 2021. *National Veterans Memorial and Museum.* [online] Available at: <https://nationalvmm.org/korean-war-battle-of-pork-chop-hill-hill-255/>

celebrates honored traditions. My father always spoke of being part of Navy "Landing Parties," He performed various functions from assisting in beachhead operations at Inchon and calling in naval gunfire at Pork Chop Hill. According to "Sailors as Infantry in the U.S. Navy" from the Naval History and Heritage Command, Navy landing parties considered some professions of Navy sailors to have a mission as infantrymen and that these bluejackets, with proper organization and training, to be as proficient as marines[11]. Regardless, dad was a monster in many forms, and we all feared him in many ways but knew he loved us.

Dad had a huge drinking problem. I remember we went to a house party at one of his friends before Christmas, and he had too much to drink. He drove drunk at a high rate of speed, hit a cattle guard, and got a flat tire. Some guy stopped by to help, and dad just knocked him out flat. Mom could

---

[11] History.navy.mil. 2021. *Sailors as Infantry in the US Navy*. [online] Available at: <https://www.history.navy.mil/research/library/online-reading-room/title-list-alphabetically/s/sailors-as-infantry-us-navy.html>

not talk to him or reason with him at all. I remember he just wanted another drink. Mom tried to reason with dad, but he didn't have it. Dad ordered us, kids, to sit on the couch while he and mom discussed the issue at hand. We sat as we watched mom and dad argue about his drinking problem. Mom tried to use all her tools, calmly talking to him. She said, "Come, honey, it's going to be Christmas, and the kids want to open their presents; let's make it a good day for the family." He started to smash the gifts under the Christmas tree in a Hulk-like fashion in an angry tantrum. As a little boy, I clearly remember seeing a candy cane bowl filled with Christmas candy in it. It was a gift for all us kids, and as a kid, it was VERY hard not to try and take candy from the bowl or eat it. Every day I would pass by, I couldn't wait to try it out. I was excited for Christmas to come. My brother and sister started to cry, and my tunnel vision was on that candy bowl. It was my little space of happiness.

When my dad started to reach for the bowl, I ran to grab it from him. I didn't want him to destroy the most beautiful thing I saw under the tree. He slapped me across the room like I was a rag doll. Mom stepped in like a Tigress. The battle was on. Mom had two black eyes, and dad cried himself to sleep. The next morning dad woke to the destruction and devastation he caused and looked for my mom in panic and sorrow. Mom and dad resolved the drinking issue, and dad never touched a drop of alcohol until the day he died in 2011. From this experience, I learned monsters could change, and they must want to change.

Our own Guardian Angel!

In my eyes, my mother is an Angel in heaven, and those who knew her on earth will speak the same. Mom described herself as a rebel; when she was in school, all the girls went crazy over Elvis and Bobby Darin. Mom made it clear she loved Paul Anka. She thought differently from everyone in her social groups. Mom was always daring to do something and start a new trend. One day I was curious and had mom take a Briggs Meyers Personality test. Sure enough, mom's letters are ISFJ (Introvert, Sensing, Feeling, Judging), the same personality as Mother Teresa. ISFJ Personality Types are known for their Sensing preference and profound respect

for facts. They tend to have a very practical
and realistic respect for facts, and their
preference leads them to store lots of
concrete information[12]. Mom was there for
dad in every crisis, protecting us kids from
his monsters. MOM was dad's rock; she
handled the money and did it well. Years
later, the family was scared if mom passed
away before dad. We all firmly believed dad
would commit suicide by a cop because he
couldn't handle life without her. Their bond
was just so close and strong. It is tough to
describe unless you have been there. It was
Devotion, and LOVE like Mother Teresa
would help the weak, sick, and poor. Mom
was there to take care of the family. My
mom was only 4'10" and full of life. She
would go head-to-head with dad and not
fear him like other people. She was the only
person who could calm dad down. But mom
was not free of demons either. One day,
years later, mom had to have an x-ray after
hitting her arm in a fall. The radiologist

---

[12] Career Assessment Site. 2021. *Celebrity
Personality Types | MBTI ISFJ Types | Career
Assessment Site*. [online] Available at:
<https://careerassessmentsite.com/celebrity-
personality-types/mbti-isfj/>

came out and told mom, with dad next to her, "There is an old bullet still lodged in your arm." Years later, we would hear of mom's story. Some drunk man tried to kill her, and he told her to get a mason jar full of corn whisky on a small table. He pointed a small pistol at her, shot, and missed. The bullet hit her in the arm, and all she could remember was his glassy eyes, him crying, and his shaking hands at that moment. Instead of killing mom, he dropped her off at the Albuquerque Indian School run by the Catholic nuns. Later on, mom would become a ward of the state and was sent to a foster home in Laguna Pueblo in the village of Puguate, New Mexico, until she met dad in Denver for her kidney transplant.

We were ALWAYS moving; mom and dad rented from house to house and took us, kids, everywhere with them. We were living in a small old adobe house in the community of Rio Chama in Northern NM when one of the family's friends brought two bushels of apricots. Dad and mom didn't have much money. They were renting, raising three kids, and had to provide utilities, food, etc. One day came;

dad brought two big boxes of mason jars and brought them into the kitchen. Upon sight of them, Mom froze in an instant! Mom turned white as a ghost and started trembling in fear and started crying like a kid and just saying "no, no" over and over. Dad didn't understand, and they sent us kids out, and they talked like they do in the bathroom. I had to go in for some water, and I remember dad talking mom into battling her demons. Dad coached her through, and mom eventually picked up mason jars and said canning food was one of her happiest hobbies when we all lived together in that house. Mom made jellies, canned salmon, preserved whole veggies and fruits. We had our own store of supplies; we were happy being poor. We did not grow up with a lot of money, but we did grow up knowing that mental illness is the norm and accepted with badges of honor. We, as a family, grew up with a firm definition of LOVE and dedication to FAMILY.

Due to mom's experience at the Albuquerque Indian School about her clothes, she was obsessed with making sure our clothes were clean and neat. She sewed up holes in our socks by using a burnt light bulb to repair socks with a needle and thread if she noticed them having holes. Mom had a rule: we had our "school clothes" and our "house clothes." Our school clothes were newer, clean, pressed, and had no holes. We changed out of our school clothes when we got home from school into home clothes. Home clothes are the ones we used to work and perform daily chores such as chopping wood and tending to horses and animals. When we woke, we would wear the same clothes from the prior cause that is how the poor people in mom's generation dressed. One day my brother and I started to alternate the school clothes and give the resemblance we were wearing a fresh set of clothes every day while at school. Mom noticed instantly, and she asked us why we were doing that.

With our heads down, I said, "The kids at school are teasing us because we wear the same clothes two days in a row." Mom clearly knew what it felt like to be teased in school. BAMO! Mom washed clothes every day and took them to the clothesline to dry, iron our clothes, and still cooked and cleaned around the house. So, because we were poor, mom made our clothes and loved doing it. She had an old German-made sewing machine from the 1950s, and it still works to this day.

In junior high, gym class was part of my schedule, and I needed some gym shorts. All the kids had their store-bought brand name or second-hand me down gym shorts. One day I lent a family friend my gym shorts. I gave him the combination to my locker, and he put them on. I was a lean kid, and he was a bit chunkier, and the way gym shorts fit him, it was obvious they were homemade. The kids teased him that day; mom found out when his parents laughed and discussed it at the table. Mom laughed as well, but she felt some shame. His parents knew we were poor and laughed at their son's experience. She collected and saved enough S&H green stamps to buy gym shorts for myself and my brother for jr. high and high school. Clearly, mom's past had an effect on her raising us kids. She had some monsters in her head, just like all of us.

While living in Rio Chama, I remember mom telling dad she was pregnant. Mom and dad always took their precautions, and neither one believed in abortion. My mom has had a kidney transplant since 1967 and is about to stress her kidney, and it became a real threat to her life, the family, and fed into dad's fear of losing his life partner. The monsters came out, but dad started to focus his anger on objects instead of us kids. He split wood, he worked himself tired, and it was a relief, but still, the monsters were there and always lingering. So now we were a family of 6, raised on dad's military pension from the VA and Social Security Disability Benefits. One day mom and dad decided to buy a house using his VA loan. The house was a beautiful ranch-style house on the side of the highway in Chili, NM. Many people would always be in awe of the old Adobe Ranch-style house. As we grew older, the family made all kinds of additional improvements on it. It was mom and dad's dream home; it became the sanctuary for the whole family. To this day, all the grandkids have fond memories of the house. Little did I know the house would cause an unforeseeable issue.

Middle Brother

My younger brother was very different from me. He served in the Army as a U.S. Army Ranger and later on to the 1st Special Forces in Ft Bragg, NC. In my brother's book, A Warrior's Path: Lessons in leadership, he describes me as a bookworm and a constant thinker. He describes himself as a rebel, being outside all the time and always having to learn for himself. I could tell him something, he wouldn't listen, and there he goes. He dealt with his own issues and may have used his military style of the decision-making process to resolve his issues. He winds up having a massive stroke in 2019 and is still slowly recovering from that.

The Sister

Our sister is very much like mom, caring, nurturing, and thinking of others. She is always willing to help and will stop at no bounds. She, too, served in the U.S. Army as a Field Medic. All of us brothers have a special bond with our sister. We all talk to her about many things. We often talk about our experiences in the Army and how some things are linked to our mental health. Today she is attending school to be a Nurse Practitioner in Psychiatry.

The Youngest One

Our youngest brother was quite different from all of us kids. He also served in the US Army as an infantryman stationed in Fort Polk, Louisiana. By 1989 would be alone in the house with mom and dad, and the monsters included. Like no other, he was a rebel, he burned part of the high school down once. Because of the incident, he was expelled from school. Our sister paid for private school out of her kindness to ensure he had an education. Later, he would be diagnosed with Paranoid Schizophrenia and PTSD then became 100% disabled by the VA. In some ways, he was just like our dad. He battled back and forth with his mental illness and would turn to self-medicating when he was off his meds.

He was constantly battling with his monsters and fueled their existence with alcohol and drugs. He would use our mom's special bond to take her money and other things to fuel his addiction. One day he was court-ordered by a judge to stop his drug use and comply with VA's medical advice regarding his mental illness. He clearly was a threat to himself, his family, and others around him. His monsters loved guns, alcohol, drugs, rock and roll, and he was not scared to flaunt and use either. When he was on his meds, it was great. We loved his jokes; his smile was addicting. He was the brother we all knew. Laughing, loving, he would give his shirt on his back if it could help a stranger without a second thought. The threat from the court order worked for a while, and then he stopped with the compliance. There was ALWAYS an issue when the family tried to enforce the court mandate. The date has expired, the police can't enforce it, he hasn't done any harm to anyone yet, we can name them all for reasons to avoid mandated help.

One day I was going to take him to the VA to get some help, and he attacked me. That was the proof we needed to have him committed. The police showed up at the scene with me holding him down and detaining him. The officer asked if I wanted to press charges, I said "No". We showed him the court order, and he was taken to the ER. An hour later, he was at his house laughing at my sister and me because he played the system. He was saying, "Ha ha ha, the doctors say there is nothing wrong with me." The police dropped him off and failed to let the ER examining doctor know that he had just attacked someone and was court-ordered to the VA Psychiatry. Every time the Doctors started to evaluate him, he was lucid and clarified all his questions. In his mind, his skewed world is REAL where he sees demons and aliens. It is normal for him, and it is combined with ours. We cannot understand nor see what his mind and eyes see together. But, everything he sees and hears is real to him and only him. Here is a simple dialogue with an Emergency Room Doctor:

Dr: Are you having thoughts of suicide?

Brother: No, Ma'am or No sir!

Dr: What brings you here?

Brother: I don't know. I just like to dabble in illegal stuff sometimes.

Dr: Is there anything troubling you? Anything you see that isn't there or true?

Brother: no, everything is normal and fine for me.

Yadda yadda

One evening shortly after that incident, he was at Mom's house and stayed awake all night with a flashlight flashing at the walls looking at the reflections trying to catch a demon. When we didn't feed into his paranoia, he stopped trying to show us his demons or aliens. When we disagreed with him, he would say, "you're an alien too," or "they got to you too, huh." He did not like Cops at all. He had a history with them and said to others, "I prefer the cops not get involved," I think their shiny badges did something to him. To him, all monsters are visible, and he is surviving in his world, struggling to keep it together, his version of sanity. He covered his phone with foil, and he was constantly buying new phones because someone was spying on him, and we can go on with the paranoia. Everyone spent exhausting hours trying to get the doctors to do something; the only advice was to call the police. To this day, I am so frustrated with a system that criminalizes mental illness and fails to

protect the masses. My brother was NOT a
criminal; he had a mental health condition.
He's mandated to take his meds to protect
himself and the masses around him, and
that fails too.

Feb 20th, 2021, the day before my
birthday, I finally convinced him to see a
doctor. His son picked him up and took him
to the VA hospital. His son dropped him off,
and he went into the ER and waved at his
son like all the other times when he would
get clean and clear his monsters out. We
were all relieved; he finally got some help;
we can all stop worrying about him. All the
relieving thoughts in our heads, "Thank god
we can rest now!", "He is going to get
better!", "He isn't going to hurt himself or
someone!", the thoughts of relief went on
and on. The next day on my birthday, I was
awakened from a nap, and my sister was
wailing "Wiz, he's gone! He's gone! They
killed him." He was walking in the street.
Screaming and yelling at things that were
real to him in a schizophrenic panic. When
Albuquerque Police Department (APD)
officers approached him and shot him eight
times as the scene was broadcasted all over
the state news channels. He was not

admitted into the VA because he was not suicidal. One of the most humiliating and devastating things to see was a loved one who fell through the system and then brutally killed in the streets.

Family

Dad had a rule about public functions, and if they couldn't take us kids, we aren't going. Many friends invited mom and dad to weddings, and if the invitation said no kids, we would not attend. Mom and dad had a sense of family like no others I have seen, and from my perspective, it was a GREAT one. But in mom and dad's definition of family, we are a whole unit, ONE. The virtue of St Francis of Assisi, "A family that prays together, stays together," was something I had seen every night before television turned off, which confused me a bit. We didn't pray together, but we loved each other in our outrageous dynamic, and things were not always bad. Like any other family, we had many great times growing up playing with friends, camping, hunting and fishing. But when there were major issues and stress, the monsters did come out. WE lived in many places growing up. For eight months, we lived in Mexico with my dad's tribe in a small town named Vicam, off the Rio Yaqui in Sonora. There we learned Spanish, and attended half a year of Mexican schooling. Dad would leave once a month to the states to get the medicines mom needed to avoid kidney rejection. We spent a whole summer in Canada in British Columbia, where we spent days playing, swimming, and fishing to our heart's content. Once again, dad would leave to pick up mom's meds and hurry back to see us having fun. Life was great, and we enjoyed it.

Dad taught us that being a man means taking responsibility for what you do and used his methods to enforce his ideals. Yes, he was mean or sadistic, playing head games with us occasionally. But dad was DAD, and we loved him as he was. He taught us to work hard and long, going into the mountains for firewood, hunting, fishing, horseback riding. He kept our brains and bodies always busy. As we got older, the house had a sense of normalcy based on dad's mood for the day. We could tell if he had a bad night or day in his eyes. We all were ready for an outrageous outburst of anger or laughter and teasing. These are just but a few stories of many, but it was HOME.

Despite my upbringing, I think America has lost a sense of the Family unit; we are all obsessed in our lives to pursue the All-American Dream. We lost sight of the fact that life is simple. I grew up in a house of mud and clay, and I am living in it right now. Yes, I grew up with monsters in the family, but I also had a lot of happy memories. We need to remove the stigma of "Manliness" and change it to something more logical. How many times have we seen a kid get into trouble? The teachers call the parents in for a conference. The response from the parent(s) is, "He is an angel at home." We as parents need to take the responsibility of listening and following through with what issues may be dwelling with our loved ones. If we can't identify the problem, we need to seek help finding and fixing it. Perversely, the school system knows more about a kid, their behavior better than the parent does. The kids spend more time in school than with busy parents at home. My dad had a saying, "Tell me who your friends are, my son, and I will tell who and what you are!"

Chapter Three

The Oldest Son

"To find yourself, think for yourself." - **Socrates**

I was born on Feb 21st in 1969, in Denver General Hospital. I am of American Indian and Spanish Heritage from New Mexico. The oldest of 4 kids and a mama's boy. My Tewa Indian Name is "Tsay Oe' Hua" Eagle Kachina, my Keres Indian name is "Hapanie Hunaste Mich Tewa," Hummingbird of the Oak clan. I am a father of 3 kids, fostered one, a grandfather to one grandson, and a proud and happy husband. At 5, I learned what magnetism was by having a family friend explain the images in a schoolbook to me. Later I learned how to multiply. So, I knew I loved learning and had constant strife to learn many things and understand how everything is connected from the top down. I am that one individual in the family who can fix almost anything, and I am given the nickname "The Wiz." In a poor household, we didn't have encyclopedias like the rich kids, nor did we have the internet back then. So, I developed my abstract way of looking from the outside in. This creativity would serve me many purposes later in life in the military, my business, and anything I could apply it to.

Carlsbad Years

In dad's later years, I heard stories from him as he grew old and feeble, barely able to stand sometimes. He would describe how he would grab us kids as babies and slam us against the wall and hold us there because we were crying too much or uncontrolled. He said it triggered memories of babies flung in the air to their deaths by bayonets he witnessed in the Korean War. Almost no one can imagine those screams and cries from a baby, the screams and cries from men and women in combat have their eerie pitch. God, I can't imagine a baby like that much more bearing witness to such an act. Dad had one huge monster on his back. I was abused as a baby by monsters and didn't know it. After those episodes, I wondered how I reacted to his touch and voice as a baby. Did I know how he caused me harm as a baby, before I was able to think and realize that what I see is truth and understanding. People in his hometown of Carlsbad feared and respected my dad due to the violent nature and destruction he could bring during a rage.

At three years old, the Vietnam War was all over the news. I can still hear Walter Cronkite say at the end of the news transmission, "And that's the way it is..." every night on CBS. My dad was a veteran, and he would receive the Veterans of Foreign Wars Magazine once a month. Just like I do with mine, I skim the pages or just place them on a coffee table or in the trash. One day when I was perhaps five years old, we received one. The magazine had military ribbons and decorations as the front cover. It had every ribbon by order of precedence from top to bottom, and I got excited as a kid. I knew I wanted to be a soldier. I heard dad telling stories all the time about the fun times in the Navy, training with his friends. I learned being a soldier was fun and noble at a young age. I wanted to be a soldier, just like the ones on the TV and VFW magazines. I asked mom if I could have the magazine with all the ribbons on it, and she asked dad. He said, "let him have the damned thing." I asked my mom for some tape. I went to the bedroom my brother and I shared. I cut the ribbons, put tape on their backs, and tapped them to my dresser. I looked at them with pride, and they were mine. I was so excited I was going to play soldier. I had ribbons just like the ones on soldiers on TV. I placed some on my shirt in random order and marched around like I had seen the soldiers march on TV. It was fun playing soldier! As I walked in to show dad, he stood up and shouted, "You know how hard it is to earn some of those, you little shit! Stop acting like those are toys! Men die for those..." the words just poured out as he proceeded to beat me with the palm of his hand. The anger just flowed from his words to the palm of his hand directly to my body.

Mom came racing in like a lioness protecting her cub; she grabbed his hands, stopped him from beating me, then told me to go to the room. She would be in the room after she talked to dad. I remember it seemed like a lifetime. Mom came in and asked me, "Why did you have those things on your clothes?" and I explained to her I was just playing soldier. She told dad, and it really made him feel bad. I was just a kid, doing what kids do. I quickly learned, some things are not games with dad's head, and those are things associated with the military and war. After mom left, I decided I wanted to pack up my clothes and go, just leave. I started to put my underwear and socks inside a bandana. I remember I asked mom what a hobo was after watching a bugs bunny cartoon. The episode had a bunch of hobos on a train, carrying a stick with their belongings tied on a bandana living fancy-free. I remember their small hats and burley faces with what looked like black smeared charcoal for beards and mustaches. Mom said, "a hobo is a homeless person, and they live by the train tracks." So, there it was. I wanted to be a hobo, getaway, and live fancy-free. As I wiped my tears away, my brother asked me what I was doing. I said, "I'm running away, and I want to be a hobo." He proceeded to find something to tie his clothes in. He decided he was mainly taking toys and socks and tied them all inside a shirt. The only issue was we couldn't find sticks long enough to sling over our shoulders, then we proceeded to laugh. Later, dad came in humble and upset and placed me on his lap and tried to explain to me in adults' terms why he got upset. I was just happy he apologized and meant it. Man, it felt so good. My hobo days ended at that moment.

My siblings and I like to laugh and talk about a lot of funny incidents occasionally. One funny incident is how mom resolved the older kids from fighting, ever. Her method was a little outrageous and somewhat amusing. Some of you may even think it is insane. But I can count only two times I fought with my younger brother with fists, and it was when we were extremely young. Mom loved music and had a collection of 45s; we just loved when she would play her oldies. When she brought the record player out, we danced and had a great time. We danced The Twist, we Mashed Potatoes, you name it, we danced it. My brother loved Chuck Berry and would walk around dancing doing his Chuck Berry duck walk. I loved Paul Revere and Raiders "Let Me" for some reason. It hit well with me when the singer would scream, "Mama! Mama! Mama!" towards the song's end. My brother and I started to fight about what was to be played next.

We started to push and shove, then throw blows. Mom stopped that; she slapped our shoulders, not hard. But I swear one of mom's slaps hurt worse than any blow from dad's monsters. We stopped instantly, mad, breathing heavily, and just fussing. She went to the Indian room and grabbed a small rope. Mom came into the living room, had me and my brother stand close together and just hug each other with arms tightly wrapped around each other. While he and I were mad, quiet, and hugging each other, she tied the small rope around us so we couldn't run or leave from that position. It wasn't tied tight or anything, it was just a simple rope. She turned off the record player, stood there watching us. She threatened to smack us again if we moved or stopped hugging each other. We stayed in place. He and I didn't want to look at each other for a few minutes. Then we got tired. Our arms were getting tired, not wanting to hug the other. Next, we started to lean on each other, swaying back and forth. When mom would notice us bickering, she told us to stop. After a few minutes, I sighed and breathed in his face, and he did the same he laughed. Almost instantly, the thought of fighting was gone at that moment and playing and laughing at each other. Mom took the rope off and told us, "You are family. We don't fight. A family stays together and leans on each other for help." To this day, we older kids have never gotten into a fight. We have always leaned on each other and been there for each other. We help each other solve each other's problems and help with each other's needs. Mom knew what it was like to be alone. Mom knew what it was like to be robbed of her childhood and family. So, I wonder today, "How the fuck did mom learn to do that?", way to go, MOM! At that point, I learned mom's small soft hand hurt when issued a punishing blow with love. Her hits had no physical pain, and the emotional pain associated was not tragic or long-lasting like pain inflicted by dad's monsters. I just love her, and the thought that I upset her made me feel bad. She always healed the pain with explanation and care. We learned and took it to heart; families don't fight. Every time I evaluate it, the answer is Family and Love. We love each other no matter what. We lean on each other no matter how far apart we are. That rope still binds us older kids together to this day.

Being American Indian (Native), mom and dad grew our hair long when we lived in Carlsbad. When it came time for school, I had to cut my long hair. I was walking into the barbershop when the barber said, "I'm sorry, but I don't cut women or little girls' hair." Mom said, "No, he's a boy." I sat in the booster seat on a barber's chair; then, he placed the small white paper around my neck and placed the barber's cape on me. I soon heard the buzz of the clippers. At first, they tickled and made my spine shiver. Then I slowly felt my hair going away as it pulled and jerked because there was so much thick hair. My hair was long because I had grown it since birth, and clippers violently removed it. It felt wrong, it just felt so wrong, it felt different! I stopped crying when the barber showed me my new look. I liked it! On the drive back home, mom asks me, "tsah moochie (my son in Keres), do you know why we had to cut your hair? Are you ok? Do you like it?" I was honest; I liked it, but I had no idea why. Mom said, "It's because, son, I don't want you to be teased by the other students when you go to school." That moment was so defining because I would soon discover something I didn't particularly appreciate being teased about at school.

So, I was glad I was going to school, playing with other kids, etc. I liked school. I liked it so much, one day it turned into a PROBLEM. It was like any normal school day before recess was about to start. I had to go poop in the bathroom. I got the teacher's permission and went into the bathroom to do my business. As soon as the recess bell rang, boys came trampling into the bathroom. They climbed on the stalls next to me and started to tease me for taking a pooh. As mom described, I quickly learned what it felt like to be teased. I did not like it!

I didn't like it one fucking bit. It would take years for me to take a poo in public. I look back on that, and I wonder. Did I inherit mom's sensitivity to being teased? Other kids being teased, to them, it didn't seem to matter, or did it? I later unlearned the "Shame" of taking a poo in public.

I liked school, and I liked it so much I talked a lot and it became a problem. While in school, I was away from home and all the monsters. I was in a classroom with other students, not in a house full of monsters and a guardian angel in it. I started talking a lot to other kids. I couldn't focus on schoolwork or the teacher's lectures. I was away from the monsters and being with other kids is just FUN!! I had great grades, but under my behavior, I had an "Unsatisfactory, Luis likes to talk a lot while in class." Mom tried to hide it from dad, but dad wouldn't have it. He called the school, asked to speak with the teacher. He told the teacher if I started to talk again, just call him, and he will handle it. One day, I finished my phonics exercise, and the teacher told me to sit down a few times. Next thing, there is a knocking on the classroom door. My teacher answers and calls me, and it's the three of us outside in the hallway. My dad asks me, "Were you talking? Did you not listen to the teacher?" I answered correctly, shaking my head. Next thing you know, the belt flies off, and I get two loud hard whacks in the hallway. The teacher screamed, "Stop it, leave!" The teacher and I go into the classroom, both crying. The kids in the class are quiet because they know what happened, they heard everything that transpired. Now it is in the open; the monsters can enter public areas, even schools. The next day a separator was placed between the kids and me until I learned to focus. The school kept the monsters away, but I could not hide from them at home. I reflect at that time, and I ask myself, "Was dad just being a disciplinarian?" It undoubtedly corrected my behavior, but his delivery and methods were way OFF. I guess he only understood violence, and violence does work well to control someone.

Living in Carlsbad, we had some great memories that I always like to reflect on. One day it was my birthday, my mom made a special cake, invited my half-sisters and my grandma (dad's mom). My parents invited many people to the birthday party because dad stopped drinking. Dad let his friends know there was no alcohol at the party. On the day of my birthday, we all waited. It seemed like an eternity to wait for everyone to show up for my birthday party. I mean to see the birthday cake, stacked cups, napkins, candles unlit on the cake, waiting for the party to start. I was excited. We were going to play, eat cake and ice cream, and dad was not drinking. When grandma showed up in her white car, dad was super happy. Dad walked her into the house with my half-sisters. All of us kids smiled at each other and they started giving us all kinds of hugs and kisses. WE love each other despite our living arrangements, and it is good just to be together. None of dad's friends showed up except for a catholic priest working with dad through his addiction, and he showed me how to multiply in my head. Dad was in shock about how many friends of his gave excuses and did not show up because there was no beer. Dad quickly severed ties with those individuals who used his friendship from his alcoholic days.

During mom's transplant days, the state of New Mexico located my mom's biological family. Mom would reconnect with her biological family because of the state searching for a sibling candidate for her transplant. I used to love going on road trips from Carlsbad to see my mom's side of the family. I mean, when the family would go on road trips all the kids would ride in the back of the truck with a camper. Every time we would pass by Camel Rock, I would get so excited cause I knew we were going to our family in San Ildefonso Pueblo. I get that childish happiness passing by that place to this day. Then we would see the foster family in Puguate, NM, and my mom's biological mom in Cochiti Pueblo. Dad and mom would just hang out and talk while all cousins would play outside. It was great!

We moved from Carlsbad to Cochiti, Pueblo, and lived there for a while. We all did our part living in the village, cleaning the irrigation ditch, participating in the cultural rites, doing things associated with pueblo Indian living. We lived close to grandma and grandpa, and our uncles were all nearby and in Puguate and San Ildefonso. One day mom and dad decided to move to Mexico and live with dad's tribe for a while. We stayed there, played with other kids. Learned Spanish, went to school. Made slingshots, hunted rabbits and birds, played in the ditches and streams. Dad and mom soon realized mom needed to be closer to a kidney doctor in the States, and once again, we moved.

We moved to Northern NM; mom

and dad knew they wanted to live near the pueblos but not on the rez. They liked their freedoms and wanted to be actual landowners, not trust owners on Bureau of Indian Affairs Trust Land on the Reservation. I remember sitting in the car in the back seat as we pulled into Espanola, NM. Dad and mom read the sign at the top of the hill as you drive north into the town of Espanola, NM. The sign reads, "Welcome to Espanola Pop 10,000." Dad looks at mom and says, "How does this small-town look, mama?" Mom said, "Yeah, I like it." She knew people nearby. We stayed in a hotel for about a week while mom and dad looked for a house to rent. To this day, I remember the intense desire to find friends and play while waiting for a home. We rented a few houses here and there until we settled in Rio Chama, NM.

I was about ten years old when I shifted how I perceived my dad and his monsters. He hadn't had a drink in many years, so there was some lower level of violence in the household. The monsters weren't totally gone; they were always there lurking. In my mind, I turned my dad into a "Robot." My dad was a robot all the time when he was mean and violent. When he was friendly, he was DAD! I don't know what made me change the way I perceived him. Perhaps it was my own self-consciousness. I knew my dad, deep down, was NOT a monster. Dad would gladly give anything he had to help his fellow man, but when dad was a monster. No one stood in his way without risk of harm and destruction. Perhaps it was my thinking that robots are only programmed to do certain functions, and as a robot, dad couldn't help it. I mean, robots can't help it, and robots can't learn anything new. Right? I was beginning to think, is this redeeming my dad because he isn't the monster he used to be. I loved him as a dad. He used to always complain with other war veterans and say, "The fucking military programs you to kill, and you don't learn to turn it off," or "They program you for war and don't deprogram you when you come back."

These were my elementary school years; we attended the local Elementary School and established some solid roots with friends through school. Though dad was a giant robot, the effect of the monsters stirred in my mind constantly. Dad used to say, "You never start a fight. Defend yourself and be sure to finish it, or I will take care of you." His logic was to make us tough, like a man.

One day I got into a fight with a fellow student. We started to push and shove. Then right out of the blue, I hit him in the face, and he felt it. I mean, that blow to his face felt so GOOD, and it was a good release for me. It felt so good and so scary at that moment. The tears started to flow. I can still hear all the kids crying my name, "Luis! Luis! Luis!"The kid I was fighting was somewhat of a bully. I was filled with adrenaline, emotionally high after I threw that punch, and I was crying hard. I started to shake in anger. I started to run away and defuse the fight. That was the only thing I knew to avoid letting my true anger out blow by blow.

One kid noticed and told me, "Luis, why are you scared to throw a punch? I saw it in your eyes." The release I felt was so scary. I knew that if I threw another punch, I would not stop. Since childhood, I had contained all the accumulated anger and pain and was afraid to let it all out at once. Afterwards, both of us boys are in the principal's office. I was standing there still crying and trying to calm down. We waited as his dad was standing there. I hear my dad walking. He sees me with tears, then turns around and walks back out the door. Later that day when I got home from school, my dad taught me what it was like to be a man. I never fought after that and avoided it for fear of releasing so much anger and hurting someone.

1981 was a defining moment for the family. Mom and dad bought a ranch-style house on the side of the highway. Dad used his VA loan to purchase the place with a very low interest rate, and it was the house everyone loved to look at when they passed by on the highway. It is a white adobe house, four bedrooms, one kitchen, one bathroom, one car garage. The roof is pitched and has red rock pumice on top, and it is so pretty sitting on the New Mexico desert sand in between two mountainous landmarks known as the Twin Warriors. For once, my brother and I had our room together, my sister had her room, and the little brother was in a crib in mom and dad's room. Over time, we all worked together as a family and placed an adobe fence around the front yard. We planted grass. We did a lot of stuff inside and out. People to this day talk about the grass and how beautiful the house looked in its heyday. The family had pride and joy in what we all built. When we gave directions to people to the house, we would say, "you know the white house with the red roof in Chili as soon as you pass the transformer?" Everyone would respond, "Oh, I love that house." or say," That house is so beautiful." Anyone in the Family could respond and say, "That is our house. That's the Trivino home." Today this house stands in huge question, as you will soon see.

Junior high was another defining moment for me. It was when all the kids from the nearby elementary schools came together in grades 7 to 8. It was fun to meet kids from Alcalde, Espanola, Chimayo, Velarde, and the list goes on from all the nearby towns. The culture in the Espanola Valley was of a lowrider culture, and most of the kids were tough. Some kids prided themselves on their family name for being a tough family. There are the Mondragon's in Rio Chama, Los Primos in Chimayo, The Padilla Brothers in El Duende. They all had a history of drinking, having a good time, and fighting. I tended to do very well in school and was placed in classes away from my friends. Then I noticed some friends started to part because I was super smart. I mean, school is about little cliques based on social status, or interest, family, and so forth.

None of my family was there, so I started to degauss my intellect. Like the daughter in the movie "I am Sam " starring Sean Penn when she downplays her intellect just to be with her dad at his level of thinking. One year the Comprehensive Test of Basic Skills (CTBS) Test placed me in the top 1 percentile of my class from my elementary school test scores. The CTBS test alienated me from my friends and my support group at school in the 7th grade. That same year, I took the test again. Instead of taking the test, I made designs with the dots on the form. In 8th grade, I was placed in substandard and average classes, and I was once again with my friends. I was no longer different in the group, and I was still smart enough to get through school. One teacher caught on and commented on my report card that stated, "Luis is a very bright student. I am afraid he just does enough to get by." Mom was always asking me why I did that. Not until I was an adult did I admit to my mom, "Because I wanted to fit in." Clearly, mom understood.

Trivino/ A Notebook of Love-My Story on Mental Health

In my freshman and sophomore years, I attended Santa Fe Indian School. I was so glad to go to a boarding school with other kids. I mean, it was an environment I was not used to living apart from everyone. But I was away from home and the monsters. In my first year, I had a roommate who was of Hopi descent and from Ohio. We stayed up all night talking the night before school, so excited for the first day of school and no one to tell us to sleep. When the Student Living Advisors (SLA) started to walk around and wake everyone up for the morning, my roommate asked if I liked to listen to music. I say, "Yeah, but all I know is what my mom and dad listened to. Oldies and Spanish Music," he said, "What about Rock and Roll?" I shrugged my shoulders and said, "A little." He had a huge cassette player and a plethora of rock and roll cassettes. The first song he Played was "Three Lock Box" by Sammy Hagar.

Just like mom in her journal

with her orange, I was mesmerized, and he started singing loud as well as we started to get showered up before we went to lunch hall for breakfast. Two days later, I was screaming and singing with him, "Suckers Walk! Money Talks! But it can't touch my three-lock box!...." He introduced me to Motley Crue, Def Leppard, many other groups, and we would sing with the player all the time. We reconnected many years later, and I soon discovered he committed suicide from his mental illness. He, too, was a veteran. I don't know what his mental illness was, but he could not hold back in saying what was on his mind and would be traumatized when rejected by women. He wasn't bad-looking either. He just said what was on his mind without regard to what he asked or stated out of curiosity.

I got my class schedule, and I selected computers for my elective. In computer class, there were about ten computers. I sat down at my desk, and the computer I had was an Apple 2e computer system. It was the latest and greatest. The teacher was a professor in advanced mathematics and did some computer programming. I learned all about hardware, software, and apple basics. My first semester in that class was bad, but I just picked things up with focus and determination. After watching the movie "War Games" with Matthew Broderick, I wondered why there wasn't a password to get into the system. So, I discovered a way to write a computer routine that placed a password on the system. I was so excited I showed the professor. He was astonished and asked me to do it to all computers in the room. It essentially prevented all the students from logging in and playing with systems during study hours. I was in advanced classes in English, Science, and I was weak in math. I should have kept up my math, I was thinking. The school had a relationship with Dartmouth College, and the science professor considered me a selected candidate to sponsor.

I loved it there at the Indian school. I was in a school where there weren't too many fights. The only issue that seemed to be of concern was who was more Indian than the other. One guy from Jemez Pueblo asked me, "What are you doing here? You don't belong here. You're not Indian." I mean, those words didn't bother me at all. I had blood relatives there in school with me. The fact that I was light skin and had green eyes made me different from my peers. Word quickly went around that I spoke fluent Spanish, which caused a stir, especially with this guy. He nicknamed me "khaki lucky" (spelled as it sounds) in the Jemez (Towa) language. It didn't bother me; I was happy and amongst people who accepted my intellect and welcomed it. The Spanish Conquistadors did not have a good history with the pueblos since the Pueblo Revolt of 1680. A period when all the pueblo people kicked the Spanish conquistadors out of New Mexico after many years of abuse upon the pueblo people.

Some 30 years later, I would call him after getting his contact information from Facebook:

Me: "Hey (his name). It's Luis Trivino, from the Indian school!"

Friend: "Who? I don't remember you."

Me: Yeah! It's Luis Trivino, Khaki Lucky."

Friend: "KHAKI LUCKY!!"

We carried on a conversation for about an hour. We talked about who we kept in contact with, who passed away, and a short version of our lives. To this day, we stay in contact, and I am still "khaki lucky" to all my Jemez friends, and I love it. At the Indian School, there were not many cliques, except the few who found refuge in drugs and alcohol. When people meet "Real Indians," we usually tend to be quiet and reserved and don't talk much. But when our walls are down, and we are amongst friends, we tend to joke a lot. One day in class, the physical science teacher asked a fellow student, "Mr. A_____ what is heat?" Mr. A_____ replied, not knowing the scientific answer with "Heat is Very hot!" The classroom busted out in laughter; it caught the teacher by surprise. After the teacher regained his composure, we continued with the lesson. At the end of the year, there was a school awards assembly. There were awards for Math, English. You name it. It was awesome to see classmates recognized. Then suddenly, the computer teacher gets up and names a few, and I hear "Luis Trivino! Most improved over the year in Computers!" I was in total shock, I liked the computers, and it was fun, and I didn't realize I had made that much progress. To hear the whole student body yell and scream in support was almost emotionally overwhelming, as I kept my secrets inside.

I was starting to do good academically and catch up, but my behavior was another question. I hung around the guys who were always into mischief, smoking weed, drinking, etc. It felt good to be a rebel, one of my uncle's childhood friends was a counselor there, and I was always in his office. It was for many minor things, spit wads, talking, you name it. My younger brother came with me in my sophomore year, and I continued my strife in academic advancement and unruly behavior. The Paolo Soleri Amphitheater was on campus, and many people played there. One night B.B King was playing, and my roommates and I went to the vehicles parked and stole a six-pack of beer. We went back to the dorm room and got a little buzzed. One of my roommates had Binaca Breath Spray and a lighter. We both started to spray torch flames at each other until I accidentally sprayed him in his eyes. He was taken to the Indian hospital, where he had 2nd-degree burns. My father was called into the school the next day, and I was expelled. My father blamed the school for my freedom and the incident. I got a severe ass beating that day. He said, "Son, you're now a man, and you can be punished like a man. If you hit back, I'm going to beat you even harder." He then proceeded to beat me with his fists hitting me hard. Every time I moved my arms to shield, a punch like a sledgehammer hit me next. I was so angry. I couldn't raise my fists in defense. I had to just stand there in the corner of the living room. As he would hit me, he would say things like, "So you want to be a man, huh!" PUNCH, "You want to embarrass me and the family that way!" BAM! I would get hit, get hit, get back up, and hear his words, "Come on! Take it like a man." Mom could not save me that day, this monster was one that mom would not interfere with, or she would get the fists too.

The bruises healed, I shrugged off the memory of that day, and my brother and I were registered into the local high school. Here, I discovered two passions, a girlfriend who I had known since elementary school and Air Force Junior Reserve Officers Training Corps (AFJROTC).

Internally I say to myself, "Wow, I get to learn all kinds of military stuff." I was bummed it wasn't a US Army-based system, but man, I was hooked. Everyone to this day associates me in high school with AFJROTC and the girlfriend I had at the time. When I see people who haven't seen me since high school, I'm always reminded with "Hey Luis, how are you doing? I haven't seen you since high school. You were in ROTC, bro, I remember you," or "hey, what happened to your girlfriend, what was her name?" In high school, I was a walking shell, even though my girlfriend was with me all the time. We shared everything, from school lockers to as many classes as possible. She was my rock, and I was hers. ROTC and my girlfriend were my passions.

Soon it came time to decide what I wanted to do once I graduated from high school. Dad and mom knew I was smart but didn't apply it much. Dad convinced himself I would make it to the United States Military Academy or the US Naval Academy.

He would tell friends I was accepted to make his words come true. We would argue about the process and how I couldn't make it to any one of those Academies. I had my beating like a man, and I was not scared to bow down much more to dad, but I knew what limit to take it to. To shut him up, I applied to West Point. I went through the whole application process. I was denied entrance due to weak academics. So, I didn't have too many options on the table, contrary to what everyone thinks, and American Indian College education is not totally paid for. Unless we attend a BIA College, which is far too few, most offer common degrees and not trendy degrees like computers. We had no idea how to apply for tuition assistance, and back then, there were no websites or people to help except school counselors. School counselors only had so much time to help the few students who did make it to college.

The 80s was a time of VHS tape rentals. I mean, everyone in town would go to Smiths in Espanola to rent tapes for a VHS player. Because we lived inside a mountain valley, TV antenna reception was almost nonexistent. We kids would love to spend time with a family we grew close to in Espanola. They had two boys. We enjoyed playing with their Atari, watching MTV from cable. We lived so rural and were so poor we could not afford those luxuries. One day dad rented a movie, "Purple Hearts," starring Ken Whal as a navy surgeon who must go on a special mission with the Military Intelligence (MI) unit in Vietnam. The scene with them training in stealth tactics and the mission was something I wanted to do. The character "Zuma," played by Cyril J. O'Reilly, was one I connected with and determined I wanted to be like him. I couldn't wait to get out of the house just to be a man.

I decided I was going to become a man in the US Army. I took the Armed Services vocational Aptitude Battery (ASVAB) test and scored average in all areas except Military Intelligence. My Spatial Perception (SP) score was off the charts, and my General Technical (GT) was substandard even for the job I was offered. The army considered the SP score valuable enough for me to get a waiver to enlist for a job in Military Intelligence. I was on cloud 9. I was going into Military intelligence. I just needed to choose the right job now. Counterintelligence, interrogator, you name it they were all at my disposal. The recruiter offered me the job as "Electronic Voice Interceptor." I joined the delayed entry program, and I was going to become a real-life "Zuma." I waited for my day to depart for basic training because I wanted to get out of this fucking house.

Chapter Four

Whirlwind

> "Every action has its pleasures and its
> price." - **Socrates**

23 June 1987, I was taken in the evening to the hotel to be on standby for processing at Military Entrance Processing Station (MEPS) Albuquerque, NM. I went to the hotel; the recruiter had given me a food voucher for a meal at the hotel and a room number to go to sleep in. I never had dinner at a hotel before, much less ordered food for myself. Mom and dad told us what we could afford on the menu, and we would choose from those options. We kids would usually get hamburgers, hot dogs, those kinds of things that were family affordable if we went out to eat. I mean, this place to me was super fancy, tablecloth-covered tables, a pitcher of cold water, two forks, and spoons. WOW, I only saw this on TV. I tell myself, "Army life is going to be great,

and I'm free!" My brother found his way there too, so I offered to split my food with him. We had a plan. He would sleep on the floor, and we would walk together to MEPS the following day at 4 a.m. I see a few young guys there. They, too, looked as lost as I felt. They told me how to present the voucher to pay for dinner. One of the guys had eaten already and gave the voucher to my younger brother, and we both had our first fancy meal thanks to the United States Army. He told me he was jealous cause I got to leave. But he knew he would be next (he tells his story in his book).   We finish our meal, happy and excited because one of us will be free. As we walk to the hotel room area, we see some classmates from Espanola and Chimayo, they are all being processed the next day like us, and they have beer and cigarettes. We stayed up all night drinking, talking. My girlfriend and her best friend showed up at the hotel and surprised me. Man, I was like, wow, "This is so fucking cool. My girlfriend is here." We go into the hotel room, talk, and have our fun. But she must leave because she lied to her parents about her whereabouts and had to go back, and home was almost 2 hours away. I tell myself, "This is just like the movies. I say bye to my girlfriend before I go off to become a man, then go to war." It was all surreal.

The following day at 4:00 a.mMy brother and I walked to the MEPS station. I start signing final contracts, urinalysis tests, finish paperwork for my security clearance and background investigation for my job. My dad always talked about Airborne; he had to go to jump school for the Navy Landing Parties, went to Ft Benning, GA in the 1950s, and was paid an extra 50 bucks a month. When it came time to sign up and enlist at the MEPS, people found out I spoke Spanish and had me take the Defense Language Proficiency Test (DLPT) in Spanish. I scored a 1+1, which is proficient but not perfect. I spoke a colloquial version of Spanish left by the Conquistadores. I suddenly became a language bypass in the

Stripes for Skills program. Six months after my advanced training, I would become a Sergeant E-5. People don't normally make that rank till about 3 to 4 years in service. I was astounded looking at the pay increase I would receive. I had to choose my remaining enlistment options, and the two I wanted to choose from were Airborne or the Army College Fund. After talking to an Army guy, he convinced me to go to the Army College Fund route. He said I could request Airborne any time in school. Now I was set to go, because of the AFJROTC, I had a promotion. I was now Private First-Class Luis Trivino. We all received orders sending us to specific places for basic training.

With our plane tickets in hand, the recruiters bused us all to the Airport in Albuquerque, NM. I had never been in an airport, much less flown on an airplane; I was culture-shocked; I had no idea where to go and what to do. All I knew was the departure time. I had no idea how to navigate to the specific gate for boarding. Fortunately for me, some gal from southern NM was there and going to Ft Dix. She guided me, and I followed her to the gate. We landed at the airport for our connecting flight and went to another gate. I mean, this gal was my age, and she knew what to do, and I didn't know a damned thing. WOW, here I am, a young man, I can't find my gate in an airport, and I'm too proud to ask others for help. I listened to her, she explained how the airports all have a structure and just find a map and look at the signs, and it is easy. WOW, such a simple concept, but I was too proud to ask for help. Had she not been going to Ft Dix; I may have been delayed a day because someone would have had to treat me like an underaged passenger and take me by hand to my plane ride.

We finally landed at Newark Airport in New Jersey; this airport was so large, and there were so many people everywhere, and I was scared. Scared because I had never been to a large city by myself. I'm in the concrete jungle, I'm a simple northern New Mexican boy who knows nothing and is trying to be a man in a far-off place. Then suddenly the large gaggle of people that reminded me of a pile of ants simmered down to just a few hundred young people on standby to get on the buses headed to Ft Dix. The buses arrived around 9 p.m.; four huge Greyhound buses picked up basic trainees and headed to Fort Dix, NJ. These buses drove what seemed 2 hours around and around Ft Dix, perhaps to ruin our orientation. We all get down, get sent to a big briefing room and we are briefed on many things. We are sent to a room where an amnesty box is to leave any illegal items and contraband listed, such as cigarettes, guns, drugs, alcohol, etc. Once we have been verified, briefed, and fed a snack, we go to the In-Processing Station. We are given a blanket, pillow, and that's it. When joining the Army, there is a list of things one must take, including running shoes, razor, padlock, or combination lock, etc. So, we locked our stuff in a wall locker that was standing alongside an assigned bunk.

The next day we were all woken up and split up in small groups with a roster number, an alphabetic character, and a number to follow. Mine was A76. We had to shower, clean up, make our beds, and clean the barracks. Then we would eat breakfast. As soon as we finished, we had to sit on a bleacher in the back and wait for roll call. Once everyone was accounted for, we would start our processing; we had our medical records made, our personnel records made, financial records made. Being so poor, I had 100 dollars of my military paycheck sent home to help my family.

The next day I got a haircut. We all lined up laughing as each guy went in with a full lock of hair and came out with nothing. We had our pictures taken, and our Military IDs made, we were issued name tags that we had to carry, and then walked over to the uniform place. We were given a green laundry bag, and we would walk in a file, and people would look at us and throw in some clothes. We moved to another line where we had another laundry bag. They put our name tags , Battle Dress Uniform (BDU) shirts, and field jackets in the laundry bag. The Cadre instructed us to write the first letter of our last name followed by the last four of our social security numbers. I never knew my social security number, growing up I never really needed to do anything with it. Trying to memorize it in a short time with all the stresses of people yelling at you where to go presented a big problem, and these people weren't drill sergeants. I was so out of my element I just followed what everyone was doing. My lowrider accent associated me with the people from the Espanola Valley. When I spoke to someone, they always asked where I was from, "I'm from Espanola, New Mexico." The accent is best described and demonstrated by some "Vatos Locos" interviewed in the MTV News clip on YouTube about the Lowrider Capital of the

United States by Kurt Loder[13].

The next day we received our battle dress shirts. I remember the cadre were yelling all the letters and numbers. Then I heard mine "T...." the last four of my social. I looked inside the shirts and jackets we handed in the day before now have our name tags sewn on and US Army on the other side. Once again, more laundry bags, and we are headed to the Central Issue Facility (CIF), with laundry bags in tow. CIF is where we get issued all the combat gear such as ammo pouches, rucksacks, etc. We simply walk in a line as people throw stuff in the bags. I mean, we are walking like robots everywhere. Suddenly, we get to the ammo pouches, and the guy is asking everyone, "where are you from?" if someone said NYC, he would respond, "The Big Apple!" guys from small towns he didn't know their

---

[13] Youtube.com. 2021. *Espanola New Mexico Lowrider Capital of the World*. [online] Available at: <https://www.youtube.com/watch?v=7z4Usl_uYul&t=10s>

nickname or popular purpose. Suddenly it was my turn, he asked me where I was from, and I responded, "Espanola NM." He put his fist in the air and said loudly, "Lowrider City!" I was like, wow and responded out of reaction, "Orale' bro!" meaning right on brother in Espanola slang. The next thing I knew, people were asking me, "What is a low rider?" They were asking me all kinds of questions. I had to explain to some people that the bugs bunny cartoons reflect real places and things. Explaining that the Roadrunner is a real bird was the biggest laugh and that turning left at Albuquerque was someplace real.

The next day, trainees requiring security clearance paperwork had to stay in a special dorm and wait for our interviews for our background investigation. In the meantime, everyone else we shared five days with got bused off to their training unit and area. There were like 5 of us: an interrogator, two order of battle analysts, one counterintelligence, and me, the voice interceptor. Once we finished, we were bussed to other locations and barracks, and we were instructed to wait with our duffle bags and combat gear. Then out the doors came the Drill Sergeants, screaming at us to get on the Semi-trailers that look like the ones used for transporting livestock. They are called "Cattle Cars." Their sharp stares, big muscles, loud voices put a scare into anyone!

We were bused to our training area, where we spent the next 11 weeks learning basic military skills such as marksmanship, military structure, operating radios, first aid, and CPR. You name it, we learned quickly and fast with the motivation of exercise and muscle failure. By mid-morning every muscle in our young bodies was sore and aching. I joined the Army weighing 119 pounds and graduated at 145 pounds. Pants that were too tight for those in the beginning now fit. The clothes like mine that were too big in the waist and shoulders now fit. WOW, all that in 11 weeks.

In all the chaos, the theme is to stick with your battle buddy and always remain a two-person team. Never break the rule. The rule is embedded in us. We use this rule in combat, training, and daily soldering. This rule sticks with us even after we leave the Army. I have seen fellow friends seek a battle buddy when a spouse or loved one is not with them in a stressful situation. A trained Veteran tends to look for a battle buddy out of instinct and reaction. Worse, when a spouse says they are leaving, it triggers the rule by instinct that we won't accept the other leaving. Is this what my dad meant by deprogramming?

After 11 weeks, I performed basic soldier skills, and I knew when to talk to someone and shut up and listen. It was much like home without the beatings. "This is going to be a breeze," I tell myself. I learned how to navigate an airport. I was a young man who graduated from Basic Training!

I then had orders to attend

Trivino/ A Notebook of Love-My Story on Mental Health

Advanced Individual Training (AIT) at Goodfellow Air Force Base in San Angelo, Texas. The job required typing skills, so I had to learn to type 25 words a minute accurately and without looking at the keyboard. This task proved extremely difficult because we didn't have a typewriter at home. I mean, in high school, my elective was AFJROTC, not typing. We are in class a lot, and classes run 24 hours a day; when a group finishes, another group goes in. The majority of everyone typed out of the typing class within a week. The typewriters in the classroom were black, and all the keys were covered with black paint and tape. I had to type a phrase, look at the keyboard layout poster on the wall, make the location by association, and hit the key. I memorized all the text in the four papers used for the typing test. Every day I looked at the poster, hunted and pecked the correct key. In class, I was given the nickname "Rock." My classmates laughed and associated me with the painted white rocks around the flagpole that never leave.

Trivino/ A Notebook of Love-My Story on Mental Health

My battle buddies were going to be flagpole and rocks, we all laughed. Before or after class, I had to go to the typing room and test. I stayed in the typing class till about two weeks before graduation. To this day, I don't know if the instructor felt sorry for me or if I truly passed because it was so intense. On graduation day, we have our military Intelligence Corps crest pinned on our uniforms by our instructors or family members. I had no family there, so my instructor asked me, "Where are you going to, Trivino?" I said, "29th MI Combat Electronic Warfare Intelligence (CEWI) Battalion, Panama." He said, "WOW! way to go, be sure to wear trojan and two-ply."

Once again, it is another airport, another bus, another shuttle, and another processing station. Another CIF, more records updates, more shots one more week in-processing into the country. I get to my unit on the Atlantic side of the Panama Canal in Fort Davis. The place mainly consists of a Naval Intelligence group,

Trivino/ A Notebook of Love-My Story on Mental Health

Military Police, Boat Transportation Company, 7th Special Forces (SF) Group, 747 Military Intelligence Battalion, 29 MI BN (CEWI), and other smaller units. The Atlantic side is so hot, humid and has about 70% humidity all the time. We would place our wallets in zip lock bags due to the amount of rainfall in the area. When we pay with cash, the money is so wet and moist it is flimsy and has a certain moist smell to it. Processing at Fort Davis meant another trip to CIF. Everyone usually had a small amount of stuff assigned to them. Not the 7th SF Group guys and the 29th MI BN. We were issued extra jungle boots, large rucksacks, and lots of combat gear. At the end of my first day there, the First Sgt provides a safety brief on a Friday and payday. The first words out of his mouth were, "None of you bastards go about injecting your dick with cocaine. Apparently, some joe did that and lost his pecker, fingers, and toes..." he goes on about other things to be aware of during the payday weekend. All these guys had Jump wings, Air Assault wings, many

other badges from tough courses in the
military. Some had Ranger tabs unheard of
if you are not in a combat arms job and
enlisted.

This unit did rotations in El Salvador,
Honduras, training exercises and live
missions supporting the US Army Southern
Command and the US Army South, and
sometimes Special Operations Command's
(SOCOM) intelligence needs for all Latin
America. WOW!! I was in a real man's unit.
We had our helicopter landing pad in front
of the barracks, and the 7th SF Group had
theirs behind their barracks. All night or
day, some team was going out to chopper
to fly somewhere, or the Naval Special
Warfare Boat Unit at Rodman Naval station
on the Pacific side. I was assigned to A
company Signals Intelligence (SIGINT)
platoon and placed on a Low-Level Voice
Intercept Team (LLVI). The Non-commission
Officers all found out I was a stripe for skills
soldier and just put me down. They hated
the program, "you're not going to make it!"

Trivino/ A Notebook of Love-My Story on Mental Health

I convinced myself it was better to earn my stripes in the unit, and I denied them. I learned so much stuff, field-expedient antennas, and set up many types of tactical intelligence-based systems to gather intelligence. Unfortunately, I cannot say much about our methods of deriving intelligence and sources, but LLVI did a lot. It was a small team of "Zumas" but carrying more than 100 pounds of radio equipment, batteries, water, and a limited supply of ammo. Much like the SF guys, they had about 125 lbs. of gear in their rucksack, not counting their basic combat load.

We were constantly in the field muddy, sweaty, tired, and had fun being a man. Right across from the Helicopter landing field was the Ft Davis NCO Club. It quickly became known that the only guys fighting in the club were the SF guys and the 29th MI Bn. One big, tall 7th group SF chief warrant officer known as "Smokey" ruled the place for sure, and I got my ass beat by him a couple of times for being a cocky and an arrogant little shit, but I loved the guy. Every time I got into a fight, I just relieved my built-up anger from all my years living in the household with dad. When I got hit, I didn't feel the pain, just like when I got my ass handed to me by my dad.

In the unit the LLVI were a special group of friends, and we called each other by nicknames, Sapo (frog in Spanish), Ole Puerto Rican One (OPO), Ole Bichote one (OBO), Yonny, Dangerous Dan, Egbert, Piolin, the battle buddy list goes on. My nickname was Ole Tiny Crazy Mexican One (OTCMO) because I did a lot of spontaneous, crazy stuff. One day the whole unit deployed to Empire range for a week and forgot about us LLVI guys in the field. When we came back from a mission, there was no one around, so we called ourselves the "Lost Boys." The lost boys were all LLVI, hard hitters, in shape, and not afraid to go out on a mission. We all still communicate and support each other through our dry and vulgar humor.

Once I got all my anger out of me and no longer feared beating someone to death, I started to change. One night I had the Panamanian bartender buy me a drink because four guys tried to jump me at the bar, and I just punched away. The Military Police came in and saw me and headed to me right away because I was usually escorted out regularly and banned for a week. This time the bartender was yelling and pointing at me, "He did nothing!" repeatedly. The bartender had seen this little, tiny guy stand his ground against four guys and won. He gave me a free shot of tequila and told me, "Tu eres un hombre." (Spanish for you're a man). I don't know if I felt proud or not. I was just numb from the physical pain and full of alcohol. I started to feel this loneliness as if I was constantly sad. I had no idea what made me feel so sad; there was nothing to be sorry about in Panama. I would walk around in a lonely shell doing crazy shit and always wearing a smile. This lonely feeling confused and shamed me. I never called or wrote a letter home during this time. I avoided my family for a year. It's weird somehow; I felt I was having fun, and My siblings weren't. I just felt they needed to be happy too. The Panamanian crisis was ongoing with Manuel Noriega in control of the country as he publicly declared war on America. Because I didn't write home much, one day my platoon sergeant received a red cross message from my worried mom. He sat down in front of me and forced me to write a letter home.

I started to drink heavily. After some time in Panama, the Lost Boys became accustomed to small and low-intensity conflicts and skirmishes all over Latin America. The first time you see someone get hit with a bullet, the sounds, smells, and noises always stay with you. I mean, once we knew of a team coming from the field or mission, we had bandolier straps filled with beer waiting for them as they came in the barracks day room, or in someone's room. The main place we loved to party was

OBO's room, he had the kick-ass Bose system. Then it was off to the NCO club. I liked the rush so much I got permission from my company commander to go out with Ground Surveillance Radar (GRS) teams in B company. So, I am spending my weekends learning how to lay sensor belts and small radar systems, once again involved in nightly firefights and skirmishes. My issues were compounding; I was dreaming wild, vivid dreams and nightmares at night, mixed with images from PTSD. One day a platoon sergeant asked me where an antenna went that was unaccounted for, and he was responsible for it. I told him it was a specific outpost on Fort Clayton. He snapped back at me and said, "The fuck it is! No one knows!" WOW, this guy was someone I idolized, and he snapped and cracked at me. I was so hurt I had to hold the tears back. The emotions sitting were so deep. I didn't know what was happening to me. As I reflect on that now, I can see I was perhaps a borderline subject of some sort. I can still remember the fear, shame, and embarrassment it made me feel. As I sit here, I wonder, wow did I do that to my wife once too many times. I never yelled or screamed at her. I mean, we always talked things through. MAN! I'm fucking screwed!!!

My alcohol became so much of a problem that the senior enlisted asked if I would be a drunk Indian again for the weekend. When I turned down sergeant stripes, I was drinking, and I was demoted twice. The second time I was sent to an Army drug and alcohol class, I learned why I felt guilty the next morning after a night of drinking. I learned I should NOT drink ever when something is bothering me. That rule has played out so well for me to this day. I often advise friends who want to stop their need to get rid of that feeling after a night of drinking. I decided to try and focus on something new. I tried learning to play the guitar for a while and often fantasized about being like Randy Rhoads; I had his posters in my barrack's room walls everywhere. I tried till it became an obsession, and I was starting to think I may have been him in some other life. Yeah really.

I tried to figure out what the fuck was going on in my head, I decided to start biking, and that worked for me. I was biking from Ft Davis to Ft Sherman (about 10 miles) and relaxing on the beach for the day. I was biking every weekend. I biked late at night when I couldn't sleep; slowly, my emotions simmered down. I would party with the guys. I controlled the volume and my pace and never drank when something negative was on my mind. I learned I was starting to control and manipulate my self-conscious thought by using little, tiny exercises to cancel the negative by trying to erase it or replace it with something positive.

I started to take control of my mental issues; I didn't go to a doctor about them. It could affect my clearance and job, then what would I do? It was something that laid heavy on my mind. Was I the only one who thought like that? I mean, we were all tough guys, and those SF guys were super knee-deep in the shit while we each performed our specific functions to support them. My next obsession was sex and women. I felt I needed to do something. I clearly understood what my instructor at Goodfellow AFB stated, "Use Trojan, two-ply." Many Panamanian women want to find an American husband and get a better life with true freedoms and benefits. Some families encouraged their daughters to find an American man. The women in Panama would sit on bleachers at the gate entrance to any military installation. They would sit waiting for any American soldier to sign them in on the post. There were so many women of all shapes, sizes, colors that we called it the "Meat Market." Man, I fit in so well. I was young, decent-looking, green eyes, light-skinned, and I spoke the language. I never signed a gal in on the military installation, and I didn't want the responsibility to ensure they left at curfew.

I would steal them from other guys or pull them away when no one was looking and flirt and talk to them. Most of the lost boys were single, and we would hang out with the Ground Surveillance Radar (GSR) guys nicknamed Lurch, the Vanilla Gorilla, and Ronbo. We all had so much fun, sex, fights, alcohol, rock & roll, it was wild. I loved it; the sex was wild, fun, and soon that satisfaction lost its taste. I started to get the empty shell back, and I was not fond of that feeling at all. I had to change. I focused on positive activities that made me feel better, and I finally got rid of the shell of sorrow and guilt. To this day, I have not felt that feeling at all. Thank God.

Panama was a lot of fun; despite all the craziness going on in Latin America, there were many fun things to do. Every Martin Luther King weekend, there was a large softball tournament that went on almost 24 hours a day for the four-day weekend. Lee Greenwood performed at Ft Davis one summer, and a good friend of mine just had a baby boy. She had me hold him so she could get a beer. When she came back and looked up, she noticed Lee Greenwood had grabbed him on stage and started to sing the Proud to be an American Song. We would reconnect years later, and she would tragically lose a daughter to her mental illness, and it just hurts so much cause this ole country gal is one of the greatest sweethearts around.

December 1989, the Panamanian crisis finally came to a head, and it was off to war. The lost boys were one of the most requested assets in the theater. We had a part in Operation Acid Gambit, Taskforce Red at Rio Hato with the 2nd 75th Rangers, the initial hit and attack on presidential headquarters called "La Comandancia." The initial wave was so fast and intense we would resize and refit with food, batteries and water. We are still carrying 120 lbs. Many hellish and nightmarish things happen in war, and there is nothing good to talk about when seeing another human suffer, scream, and die. Being a soldier is complicated and comes with many sacrifices and compromises. If asked to do it again, I would go in a heartbeat. We do it for the guy standing next to us, and sometimes it's hard for someone to understand.

Experiences in Panama defined all the lost boys, including myself. I think that is what keeps us together to this day; our mental health depends on knowing another lost boy is not "lost" again. Years later, I would wind up helping Yonny with a VA claim for PTSD. The VA Dr. said a lot of what he was saying was bull shit. He called me up one day, venting about it. I said send me a fax number. I faxed Yonny a Deposition Form (DF) written by the Company Commander stating the requirements to be on an LLVI team. It provided detailed information of whom we supported and where we operated. I also sent him copies of orders assigning us to various Operational Detachments Alfa ODA Teams to C Co 3/7th SF Group. I had saved all that stuff for some reason. That shut the fucking doctor up, and Yonny got his disability rating from the VA. Panama was my first Army assignment, and it caused me a lot of PTSD issues. The stigma among the community is to be a tough man and do your job.

The day snorkel got promoted to Sergeant, it just made me angry. Snorkel has less time in the Army and the unit than me, and I didn't understand. Why am I not being promoted? I am damned good in the field and know my job very well. I started to complain to Sapo, who was my squad leader at the time. Sapo said, "Hold it, Trivino! Do you want to know why you don't get promoted? It's because you're a fuck up! You drink, you're rebellious, you get demoted. The only place for Trivino is in the field, and the leadership wants to promote you, but you FUCK UP!" I was like, WOW, I needed to hear that. I shut up and thanked him and just sat down inside my room that evening, thinking about everything I had done. I never considered what was going to happen when I did crazy shit. I just loved having fun and didn't consider the long-term effects of my actions. Well played Sapo, I listened and decided I needed to shape up and improve myself. I was working on improving my emotional and mental issues that I totally forgot about my professional self-image.

One day we were all called back to Ft Davis; at the end of Feb 1990, all the LLVI teams were called back to Fort Davis. The company commander stated to all of us "The Panama Canal is liberated, and the US forces had to meet the conditions of the Panama Canal Treaty." The Treaty called for a limited number of troops in the country. The company commander had to decide who he was sending back to the US quickly, and he had to decide who stayed, and we had to be packed in a week and gone. Some of us went to San Antonio, Tx, Key West, Fl, Fort Meade, MD, the Lost Boys were no longer going to be together again. The departure of friends triggered a traumatic experience for sure, and the lost boys' breakup did bring trauma to Yonny. He was no longer assigned to A company; he was doing some Human Intelligence with B co, and all he could do was see the lost boys broken apart and given orders to different destinations around the world.

Sapo, OBO, OPO, and I wound up in San Antonio, Texas, and we started to perform our job in a strategic function, no more rucksacks, field gear, etc. The new unit was a strategic unit, and we were no longer in the field getting shot at. We all had desk jobs performing our duties, perhaps a way for the Army to let us relax and tame down. The single soldiers lived in barracks on Kelly AFB, and we worked in a complex about 8 miles away on Lackland Medina Annex. This strategic job was so technically focused. The lost boys trickled into our new units looking like soldiers in recruiting posters walking in with medals on our chests. People would talk to us about our experiences. We had a company commander who was a Vietnam Veteran, and he had the opportunity to award us lost boys our medals for wartime service and accomplishments. For him, he said it was such a rare thing for a commander to do since his days in Vietnam, and he was honored to do so. MI soldiers are not combat arms, and we rarely get the recognition as those soldiers do. The person submitting for an award really can't describe what happened to impact a mission that saved the lives of 100 people or brought down a high-profile target. We don't divulge intelligence methods or sources; the awards are usually rescinded or downgraded due to lack of detail in merit. Besides, we lost boys didn't do it for the honor, but for each other and the man standing next to us. I had a new focus, and I would straighten up.

OBO and I are barracks roommates, and we are in a deep sleep. Suddenly, I hear doors slamming as people wake up, washing up, and getting ready for work. The next thing I do is yell, "In Coming!" OBO hits the concrete floor from his bed so fast like he anticipated the round was coming in short. We both look at each other like, "What the fuck!" All we did was react from training and our recent experiences. The adjustment was not going to be easy, and we knew it. We got assigned to our scheduled shift called a flight because we were on an Air Force base and they sponsored the mission. Once I started training, I realized I was not technically proficient in the strategic tasks and aspects of my job. These Air Force guys have the technical part of the job and changes perfectly planned out for training. But man, the transition from a combat posture to a strategic posture in work was the most challenging thing. We lost boys kept talking about how hard it was to learn a new target. What was extremely hard on me was the Air Force training system to measure and test for proficiency in our targeted group or area. The multi-million-dollar equipment we used belonged to the Air Force. We Army folks had to abide by their standard and ability. The amount of multitasking, concentration, time just sitting down on target placed my mind in a state of intense focus and learning what I call "Focused Automation," and it was exhausting.

As I reflect now, I started to develop my bipolar traits. I don't know if I was genetically predisposed, and all these mental exercises to comply and perform my duties awakened and heightened any Bipolar symptoms. I was in a constant mental struggle, waking up on time, shit, shower, shave, find a way to work, train, work, physical fitness formations, the list goes on and on. The only fear I had was being at the wrong place at the wrong time. Based on my experience at that time, it would get you killed.

I started to dream of being late for formation, catching a plane, late to a chopper exfil. It got so bad that I had to go to the ER and complain about my heart-thumping super-fast. I couldn't sleep no matter what. The Dr. asked me questions about my mental health. I flat outright denied having any mental issues. Hell, I just got back from a tour overseas riddled with low-intensity conflicts. I'm a man; I can handle it. I was WRONG! Deep inside, I was suffering, not from pain or loss but from the need to adjust and perform in my new tasks. Training my brain turned out to be a challenging and taxing process, but I wanted to improve or fix my mental state. Once again, the threat of losing my job and clearance or being labeled weak prevented me from seeking the help I needed. The ER doctor said I was stressed, experiencing heart palpitations, and needed rest and relief from work. Military doctors are limited in prescribing benzos, so I was given bed rest for three days. As I walked out discharged from the ER, I threw the bed rest slip into the trash and said, "Fuck this." I stayed in a manic state for about a week and slowly started to come down. I fell into a good work regimen, and things began to form a routine. After about four months, I was certified in my new job, and performing well to standard.

Sapo's marriage was falling apart, and weeks later, Saddam Hussein invaded Kuwait, and the US was starting to form a UN Coalition of troops. Word came down the line that they needed volunteers with real-world mission experience. Sapo told me about it, said he was going to volunteer and go. I responded without hesitation, "Fuck it, I'm there with you, bro," knowing weapons of mass destruction were some of Saddam's preferred tools of use. Here we go, to Ft Stewart, Georgia, two young men, experienced in combat and ready to serve again without question. Everywhere we went, the community was supporting our troops. The eerie thing for me is that the song "I'm proud to be an American" resonates with the emotions associated with death, sorrow, and fear of war, similar to taps for my father. Every veteran has some song or sound that just brings that uneasy feeling, and this song does it for me. When people ask why I hate that song, they make comments like, "Are you not proud of your service?", "Are you not American?" I just stay quiet and respond in my head, "I'm as American as they come motherfucker! Shut the Fuck up!" Sapo and I, together again from Panama to San Antonio, Texas, now to Iraq, true as two battle buddies and brothers in arms.

We got to CIF and started in-processing by getting shots, all dental records updated, the whole spiel. We had been deployed so much our shot records just needed reviewing. We already had our financial allotments set. We just needed to be assigned our gear, sent to a unit, and go. We get assigned to the 24th Military Intelligence Battalion with the 24th Infantry (Mechanized). Wow! Sapo and I have been exposed to helicopters, planes, riverboats but never tanks and tracked vehicles. "This one is going to be fun," we said as we laughed, headed to another conflict. We went to Saudi, stayed for months training and adjusting to learning the new vehicles, and I got promoted to E-5, Sapo to E-6 without the need for a promotion board, a "Field Promotion". I finally got my stripes! Sapo and I later received letters from the company commander in San Antonio, who pinned our medals on congratulating us on our promotions.

We road marched to a valley near the Iraqi border and watched as the b-52 bombers hammered the Iraqi troops. Man, those Cluster Bomb Units (CBU) are some scary shit to see, and to be in the middle of a drop is something I would truly dread. Once the ground war started, we were on our way to Iraq in a huge, massive movement of tanks, tracked vehicles, automobiles, helicopters, and you name it. Once again, the same type of atrocities. Sapo and I are used to the routine, dead bodies everywhere, burnt vehicles, burning buildings, the smell of death, oil, gun powder, the spell of explosives, yadda yadda.

All Iraq did was fine-tune my "Fight or Flight" mental psyche. During combat we track, analyze, decide, and adjust to every situation and problem at hand instantaneously. For those of you who have been around a veteran(s) in crisis. Have you noticed how we can change and adjust our decisions without hesitation? It is because we have already evaluated the situation, then adjusted the current situation based on the new information or "Intel." We apply it to everything; we are trained to suppress our emotions and make quick and decisive decisions in life-threatening situations. That is something we cannot just turn off; it is embedded in our survival "Fight or Flight" program. Once we program that area of our minds, we can't turn it on again and readjust it. The program must be running to unlearn what we already trained our minds to do. When people see me making a quick decision, they may say, "He is making a decision based on his emotions." I say wrong! In my mind, during a "fight or flight" situation, my mechanisms are awakened, trained, heightened, and reactive. It is my own defense against the unknown. It has helped other veterans and myself to just stay alive. When that response is trained in unison with a team or a unit's need for survival, we do things on instinct. We stay focused on the task.

In my attempt to unlearn my "fight or flight" program, I tend to try and use logic and a safer and slower decision process. It is hard because, as a veteran, I need to have a quick response for adjustment in my decision-making in stressful situations.

I finally convinced myself, if bullets aren't flying, I can be level-headed. But in this situation, I'm in now, I am in fear of the unknown dealing with my marriage. This problem has a great big hold on me, and I admit I am super scared. It is like I am on

Trivino/ A Notebook of Love-My Story on Mental Health

the border of "Fight or Flight" and emotional distress. I know I must slow down, and I am currently working on that.

Writing is my outlet, and I think I like it; I must stay focused.

Chapter Five

Tidal Wave
"Sometimes you put walls up not to keep people out, but to see who cares enough to break them down." - **Socrates**

Desert Storm ended, Sapo and I were sent back to San Antonio, Texas. People from our unit were waiting for us at 9:30 p.m. in the airport just to welcome us. They all had a beer, a cigar, chewing tobacco, just some of the simple things a soldier appreciates and we don't have while deployed and now we are home. Sapo is given a ride to his apartment, where his wife and daughter are. I'm headed back to the barracks and not knowing if I will have a new roommate or if OBO was still there. I get to my old room. I have a new roommate. There I see some of my stuff on his side of the room and his stuff all over my bed. I was angry! I started tearing into this guy who I have no idea who he is, what his rank is, but I told him exactly how I felt about the situation. WOW, I discovered life goes on without you when you are away, and don't expect it to be the same when you get back. Sapo soon found this out when he discovered his wife wanted a divorce, and she had spent almost all their savings while he was away.

Sapo started in his downward spiral. Here is the guy who got me into my self-improvement, and I can't help him fix this situation. I made sure to be his battle buddy in his battle with his demons and his divorce. Being promoted meant I had to move out of the barracks and into an apartment. I made sure I was in the same apartment complex where Sapo is living. I babysat his daughter. We went to the pool together, and we took his daughter to carnivals and anything to make something normal in Sapo's situation. I knew it worked for me, and it had to work for him. In the meantime, he showed me how to manage my bills, create a budget, and work on my finances while maintaining a single life as a soldier. I never knew how to manage any of those things, and the Army provided everything for me. My brother used to joke about marriage, and he would say, "If the Army doesn't issue it. I don't need it."

One night, Sapo just wanted to go to the club, and I took him, no questions asked. We chilled, he drank some, and we closed the club, the man was broken. On the way back home, he opened the car door window and just got onto the hood while I was driving 65 mph on loop 410 headed back home. There were cars around, and he was all over my hood and windshield. I couldn't tell if he was screaming or crying; he just needed to do something. I couldn't slow down due to traffic. I see he has three good points of contact, so I just let him ride his ride! He came back in, and we just didn't talk about it. To this day, we call it, "Remember when you were on the hood?"

One night we decided to go out to the

club again. Sapo decided to relax and chill out and watch me; he was the designated driver this time. He decided to chill from drinking after the car hood incident. I love music, and I love dancing with my soul involved with the music flowing through and coming out with expressions and movements. I danced with headphones in my room in Panama, in Saudi, anywhere I could. It just felt good to dance like no one was watching! I used to go to the club and just dance the night away. I'd dance with any gal who wanted to dance with me. This evening I noticed a young lady walking, and I just loved how she reacted to the music. I so badly want to dance with her. I approached her and said she was pretty, and she looked at me like I was crazy. As she started to walk away, I tried to grab her hand and tell her I was sorry I bothered her. Little did I notice she was wearing a prosthetic arm, and the arm came off with the strap when I grabbed it. In my eyes, she was whole, and I didn't see any imperfections in her at all. I see people as beautiful beings with no flaws at all. I learned to love myself and accept what I can change, but if I can, I need to change it. To this day, I wonder if I caused some traumatic event in her mind. I know what it is like to be teased about something that is a core part of me. If she ever reads this, "Please know I liked you and wanted to know you," that's all. Some people started to laugh, some people were surprised, and the poor young woman ran out of the club. I felt her shame like I was sitting on the toilet in first grade. Sapo slowed down; he found his love, and they started their courtship and, to this day, are still together going strong.

It was another club night for me after a long week of shift work. One night, a few of the guys decided to go club-hopping, and I was more than happy to go along. I saw this gal dancing while she was talking to some guy, she was around my age, and she had big boobs. I know what I like and like boobs. Just like women like guys with certain features. Just our likes truly can be insane at times, like feet or toes. I never really got into that, ha ha ha. Anyway, I stood there for a while, got her attention, and she stayed talking to the same guy. She said "wait" with a hand gesture as she smiled at me. I stood there for two songs, and then I just couldn't wait for her anymore. I asked the guy if he minded me talking to her for a minute. She looked at me, and I just picked her up over my shoulder and carried her to the dance floor. She slapped me on my back. In a way that she didn't want me to stop, I could tell by the force in her slaps and her laughing. Otherwise, I would have stopped. I gently placed her on the dance floor, and we just proceeded to dance. It was just an attraction that we both couldn't deny we danced the night away. I told her I got back into the states from Iraq. She was a medic in the U.S. Army reserve and was there with her best friend. She and her best friend were recent Licensed Practical Nurse (LPN) graduates from the Nursing school at St

Philip's College through the U.S. Army Reserve. We danced all night long, and the club started to close. I was looking for a cab when her friend decided to give me a ride. They were talking, and I was in the back seat of the car. Her best friend said, "What are you going to do?" She responded, "I'm going to take him home and have my way with him. Then take his ass to his home or drop him off somewhere." Her friend responded, "Ok, just let me know." I recognized it as a friendship as the type the lost boys possess. We both woke up the next morning as we started to just talk in bed, "What is your family like?", "How many siblings do you have?" The conversations just went on and on. There were a lot of similarities, and when we had a difference of opinion, she made hers clearly known.

      Much like Sapo when I needed to get my act together, so I figured this must be good. We took it slow, then decided to move in together. Her friends and my friends started to mingle together at small barbecues and celebrations we hosted.

My parents talked to her, I talked to her parents, and the focus from both parents was the differences in race. I guess their generation was focused on race, whereas we did not let that bother us. One day our parents decided to talk to each other. The next thing you know, our parents are fighting and cursing each other out. Her parents called her up and said, "His parents are crazy!" My parents followed suit, "Son, don't you ever have me talk to those people they're nuts!" We both held true to our promises. Our parents never ever interacted after that point.

Then my lease was up, and so was hers. We decided to save money and try to live together to see how it goes. I have had many roommates in the Army, but moving in with a woman just changes the whole dynamic and sets forth new precedence in wants and needs in the roommate relationship. If I left the toilet seat up, boy I heard about it from the other room. We certainly were working hard at it to make it work, considering our differences in doing laundry, cooking preferences, etc. It was a very hard adjustment, and this woman is not afraid to voice her opinion which made it even harder.

I came upon cap cycle, the point where it is time to change duty stations, and I'm set to go to Panama alone. It triggered fear in both of us. After time and consideration, we decided to get married and see how we could handle being married together. We got married in a small Vegas-style chapel in San Antonio, Texas, in a strip mall. The place was nice, with pews and flowers everywhere. I wore my uniform, and Sapo was one of my best men. Her parents went to San Antonio for the wedding. We had a reception, and everyone danced. My family couldn't make it due to finances, and I spoke to them before and after the ceremony.

My cap cycle got canceled, and we

stayed in San Antonio for another year. Suddenly, she calls me into the bathroom and tells me, "We are pregnant." Sure enough I saw the pregnancy test, I told my friends at work, and we just celebrated. Some people said, "Wow, can you imagine Trivino as a father?" I paid no attention and told myself I was going to be the best father I could be. Our son was born in Wilford Hall Hospital in 1995. He was the greatest thing created with a part of me. I used to just stare at him, see what features or traits he had from both of us. He was so innocent and pure!

One day I received a phone call from my dad. Mom was in the hospital after she fell on their way to meet with the school counselors and the principal. My little brother did something, and I don't really know what it was. My wife and son would fly to N.M. to support the family. We figured seeing the grandson for the first time would lighten things a bit. That evening my wife, son, and little brother were home. One of Dad's monsters came out. My dad and little brother started to discuss what had happened. Dad is stressed about mom in the hospital and not able to cope with that. All I know is it was his turn to become a man at the punches by the Hulk. I never knew this until years later, and I wonder how I would have reacted had I known.

Then the real task of parenthood came upon us. One evening our son was colic. I had come in from a swing shift. She picked up a night shift as a home health care worker. I am grateful she had the flexibility to do that when we needed extra money. Soon after she left, our son started to get colic, and I knew the signs. We were transitioning him from milk to cereals and bland foods, and his stomach did not handle the transition well. He cried and cried; I could barely stand it. I wanted to shake him and ask him why he was crying so loud. I was just tired. I wanted to sleep, but I reminded myself how dad lost control so easily, so I kept my cool. I helped him through this until he went pooh and held him until we both lay asleep on the armchair together. For me, it was the most gratifying and defining moment, and I found I can be patient and be a good dad. Growing up in my household, I was so fearful of how I could become a monster like my father through my kids' eyes. Every corner, I found myself becoming more patient and accepting of his uncontrolled need to cry or behave in a way that disturbed my own mental space. I soon heard the same people who criticized me about becoming a parent," Wow, Trivino is a great dad!" It wasn't about their criticism that made me want to change. It was about me wanting to be a good father and ensure my kids did not inherit the same type of monsters I had as a kid.

We worked on our dynamics as a couple and as parents with our son. Once again, I came upon the cap cycle for Panama. This time we were headed to

Howard Airforce Base. I remember taking my wife to a cap cycle meeting, and one guy I attended AIT with was there with his wife. She was greatly more outspoken than my wife, and it was sort of a relief. They briefed us couples on the process, then the next thing we heard was that the soldiers must fly there first, then wait for housing arrangements before dependents can arrive. My buddy and his wife were stationed there together, and she just blurted out angrily at the person briefing our couples, "WHAT! He isn't going to Panama by himself! Do you know what the women are like there!" she just kept ranting and raving. Well, that little burst does not help my marriage much. I proceeded to explain to my wife what the situation was like at the "Meat market." Next thing you know, some insecurities and doubts are coming from both sides. As we started to agree on things; then, surprised she was pregnant again. The stress just keeps piling up.

Trivino/ A Notebook of Love-My Story on Mental Health

I arrived in Panama, which means there is more in-processing again. It's a "hurry up and wait" type of situation, a normal pace for things to happen at the Army speed of things. Eventually, we get Army housing on Ft Clayton off old Colonel's row. We have a huge four-bedroom with living quarters the size of a Georgia mansion. The house is about ¼ mile from the flagpole on the post, and every morning the reveille trumpet and cannon fires off at 6 a.m., and it shakes the windows. We are within walking distance to the library, the community center, the pool, the shoppette, the NCO club, and the restaurants. This was a dream come true for a young family getting things together, but we still had our differences in parenting style. I liked to set boundaries and keep them. In my opinion, her boundaries were not consistent, and it was a tidal wave of arguments. The younger son was born in December 97, and it was constant work on my part. She eventually got a job at Gorgas Army Hospital, and we were into our normal grind; because the cost of living is low, we accepted a family as our live-in help. The husband and wife had two little girls. They helped us with the kids. The oldest was learning Spanish and their kids were learning English. It was a great big family. We loved it. Once again, like clockwork, we were pregnant again. Our daughter was born in March 1997.

Once again in compliance with the Panama Canal treaty, US Southern Command started reducing forces and our entire unit was set to relocate to the US. That means the whole unit, equipment, and aircraft all must move to one location and be permanently stationed there. My wife received a letter from the Nursing program at the University of Texas Health Science Center (UTHSC) in San Antonio saying her credit hours were running out of time. If she didn't enroll in a nursing program, she would have to start all over again. So once the unit got a place identified, we set things in motion. It turned out to be Ft Bliss, Texas, so she applied to the nursing program at the University of Texas-El Paso, and she was accepted. Then two weeks later, those orders were rescinded, and we are going to San Antonio. She cancels UTEP and applies at UTSA. She is accepted there. Bam! Those orders are rescinded, and it is back to UTEP! She was denied at UTEP because the position she had was filled after her declining entry into the program. The tidal waves kept coming and coming.

We decided on University of Texas Health Science Center (UTHSC) San Antonio, and she went stateside with the kids, arranged housing, worked full-time, and she watched the kids. Even if it was a semester, maybe I could get a compassionate reassignment from Ft Bliss to San Antonio. I was in fear and on pins and needles. Bam, another tidal wave the unit is getting ready to deploy to Bolivia; I can't deploy because I have no updated dependent care package. The wife and the kids are in San Antonio, TX, and the U.S. Army has sponsored them to be in Panama, which is where they should be. We were faced with a big decision, have her fly back and lose her path, or I get discharged, and we work this out in San Antonio. We had to make a huge decision in a short time. I started to get heart palpitations; I couldn't sleep. I was getting flashbacks while at work. I started my downward spiral. After much consideration, I chose family over the army. Some guys in the unit teased me, "Oh, the wife leaves, and you get out!" It was placed as a screensaver on a computer, but they didn't know the whole story, nor was it theirs to know. In October of 1998, I was discharged after more than ten years of service. I was at the halfway point of retirement, but I decided the Army would still be there after I was long gone. But spending time with my family is far more precious.

WOW, what a huge life-changing decision we made for the sake of family. She was already a step ahead and found a place for us to live. The plan was to use my

GI Bill and Army College fund and go to school. We made a great decision but were always conflicted when it came to the kids. I started attending a local community college and enrolled in the criminal justice program. After enrollment and V.A. confirmation, it took over a month just to get my first installment check from my GI bill, and I must maintain full-time status for the whole 800.00 a month. We agreed it was cheaper for me to be a stay-at-home dad over daycare costs for the kids. She would attend her college part-time one semester and work, and she would adjust her work schedule around my class hours.

The stress of raising three toddlers at home is a full-time job, and I believe Congress should consider the stay-at-home mom/father a full-time job because it takes a big chunk in the finances to make it work. The needs of the kids far exceed the tax break provided when sending kids to daycare on a yearly basis. It was awesome playing with the kids, stopping petty fights and disagreements. I also used the rope on my kids, and to this day, they have NEVER come down to fist throwing at each other. Thanks, MOM! After about a year, we discover the middle one has an 11-month speech delay, he can't enunciate his words properly, and when he can't communicate, he simply screams in frustration. We have no health insurance, and there are no Indian Health Services in San Antonio, and the family does not qualify for contract care from the BIA because we didn't live on the reservation. Because of his age, the middle one was able to attend special education services at the elementary school to focus on speech therapy. Before you know it, he is talking, and he won't shut up, ha ha ha. But he learned screaming is the way to react in frustration and turns out to be something he is currently working on. Great job, son. Keep up the good work!

When he started to attend school, he was diagnosed with attention deficit hyperactivity disorder (ADHD). When I took him to his first treatment session, I let him do all the talking. He explained to the Dr that his brain works fast, and he can't slow it down. That hit me like a time tidal wave. Oh my god, is he like me? Is this hereditary? Did I damage him? It bothered me so much, I lost sleep, it was a struggle trying different medications that could help him, and we didn't have medical insurance. I began to think about the security we had while I was in the Army, healthcare, housing, education and compared it to being there in our current situation.

Due to the stress I started to have nightmares, and I would wake up screaming a motor shell landed on my oldest. I'm screaming his name in bed. My fears and nightmares are starting to merge with objects in my real world. I accused my wife of cheating on me. I snapped and grabbed her by the throat, not out of hate or anger, but desperation for help. It scared her so much she called the cops, and I never blamed her. I left the house to defuse, and I just wanted to go to New Mexico and see a medicine man. I am sick from war, and maybe cultural healing will help me through this. I packed up some belongings and took a pistol with me for the long journey back to New Mexico. I was arrested at a gas station near the house, calling my parents telling them what happened. Dad already knew what caused it with only the mention of my triggers. Just a week prior, I tested for the San Antonio Police Department and was two weeks away from attending the academy. That dream is out the window due to my mental break; it didn't do much to help me. I just wanted to do my part and help, and my military transition was one of the most challenging things to go through.

      I spent a weekend in Bexar County Jail with some serious charges against me. I am evaluated medically and deemed ok to go in with the population. I cried on my jail bunk for the night just because my brain would not stop with tidal waves of thoughts and emotions. I had so much going on, a lack of sleep, and I never had the tools to adjust my reactions.

Once I got out of jail, I stayed in the house with some lost boys, Cowboy and Scotty! Cowboy became a nurse after the Army, and he helped me get the help I needed at the Vet center. The VA Psychiatrists placed me on different mixes of mood stabilizers until I found the right cocktail for my sanity without feeling like a shell to the world. The family was happy to receive me back again, and then we had to deal with the courts. We had little to no money, raising kids dealing with court fees, and now we had to get a lawyer involved. In the end, all the charges were adjudicated, but they are still on my record. Due to mental illness, I have a criminal past. She states, "Had I known it was going to come down to all this, I would not have called the police." It makes one think, who do you call? Who can help? All this financial burden and stress on the justice system and all I needed was a little help in my mental health.

We bought some land in Natalia, Texas, and placed a nice, manufactured home on the property. I continued to attend college. I changed my degree from Criminal Justice to Computer Science. The core math requirements started with Calculus 1. I was substandard in math and had to start from math 301 and work my way up, pre-algebra, college algebra, trigonometry, then calculus. Each class takes three months at a time. It took me over a year to just reach the start of my math requirement for my chosen degree. Through the help of the Vet Center and Texas veterans commission, I was able to file for V.A. disability and got a 50% rating. My college money was running out quickly, and I still had no degree. That placed a lot of strain on the marriage because it was her turn to go to college and slow down a bit from working all the time. It caused resentment on both sides; suddenly, while in college, I got the attention of a math professor who had a friend looking for a well-rounded Jr Programmer with good math skills. It turns out I had those and the experience in aerial reconnaissance missions. His friend's company was working on an Electronic Intelligence (ELINT) platform and needed some help.

Finally, I had a steady job, income, benefits, and I was still going to school. I worked 34 miles away in San Antonio, raced back to get the kids, coach them in all their sports, make sure they did their homework. When she was off, she would take them to their games while I worked on homework. It was super stressful and just super hard to maintain a marriage. We both found ourselves drifting away. I got on yahoo messenger and fell in love with the most beautiful girl ever. She was in San Antonio and from New Mexico. I added her to my yahoo friends list. She asked me, "Are you married?" I said, "Yes, but I'm not happy." she said, "Bye." I asked myself, "What the hell am I doing? I have a wife and kids."

After my G.I. Bill ran out, I attended my advanced computer science classes at UTSA. The VA helped me pay for my degree using the vocational rehab program. After about four years, I met the core math requirement for the computer science program. One day I was late for class. The college registered double the number of students, and the main parking lot was under construction. The professor was about 5 minutes into the lecture when I walked in. The professor states I'm late and I am to leave; that's his rule. I told the professor I was there on V.A. money. It was not my fault it took 35 minutes to find parking and walk to class. If he forces me out, I will complain to the V.A. that he denies me an education due to his personal rules. The VA education counselor caught wind of our verbal skirmish, called me into her office. We went over the incident, and the V.A. counselor suggested I attend St Mary's University to finish my education. The counselor was confident I would be able to pass the program since all past attempts by veterans failed in the Math requirements and I already met them.

I loved St Mary's; it was peaceful, tranquil, and trendy. It's a catholic school based upon the Marian Order of Priests, and this is where John Santikos, Bill Greehey, John Quiñones, Michele Lepe, Stuart Parker, and more outstanding people attended. This place had me take additional credit hours in Theology and Philosophy, and I am so grateful to the University for that. At the time, I did not practice my religious faith. With the education provided by Saint Mary's University, I regained my relationship with God the Father. Using my thought process applying spatial perception, I soaked in all the ethics and theories of Immanuel Kant, Socrates, Plato. We learned about Kant's Categorical Imperative. I loved it all!! In 2007 I received my bachelor's in computer science after seven years, raising kids, holding a job, marriage, and coaching the kids in all their sports.

I got a job at a start-up and wrote one of the first web-based Electronic Medical Records (EMR) systems. The site had the attention of Dr. Oz, who appears on Oprah Winfrey's show. The owner of the company is a 21-year-old genius who is trying to make it work. We get the first iteration going. Then we hit phase two, and the site is a hit. MyMedlab.com was one of the first of its kind, where people can purchase a custom series of lab tests. We graphed the progression/regression of A1C, Cholesterol. You name it, we had it with a graphical measure of time, or by values. Most of these features are expected today in Electronic Medical Records (EMR) systems. I was working and not going to school. It was great. Like a ton of bricks, the wife and I started arguing again, and I just left. I was tired of the arguing, and it was not good for the kids.

During this phase, I learned how to deal with my anger by keeping my mind focused. If it was homework, it was math.

Trivino/ A Notebook of Love-My Story on Mental Health

Mathematical problems would just relax me and place me into a realm where I could get a calculated output from an equation. I was looking for predictable positive output during this time in the marriage. After 16 years of marriage, we agreed it was best to divorce. As I look back and reflect, I spent a lot of time angry and frustrated about many things. But it took a toll on the children because we were both still sour about petty things in our arguments, and it just made for a sour recipe. Today we are friends and treat each other like friends. We resolved issues related to the kids together, continue to make them a priority. We alleviated their stress by getting along and being adults, and amicable about everything we say and do. After all, it is for the family, we may not be married, but the kids are still ours and our FAMILY.

The thought that a mental illness can be hereditary and triggered is always a threat that does not discriminate. AMI can hit anyone at any time. It doesn't care about wealth, health, social status; it just appears.

I still say, "Accept the Disorder, Love the Person." Just like I love my wife.

Chapter Six

My Notebook Love

"One word frees us of all the weight and pain in life, that word is Love" - Socrates

It is 2007. After a 16-year marriage, I am alone in a small one-bedroom efficiency apartment in San Antonio, Texas. This apartment is tiny. The living room and kitchen are connected, there is no room for a small kitchen table, and the bathroom is in the bedroom. I am taking it one day at a time, attending counseling sessions at the VA hospital. The psychiatrists have prescribed me a cocktail of medicines that I take daily. Right now, they make me feel like a shell of a person showing little emotion, but I am lucid, stable, and slow to think.

I get home from work and get back on my computer to keep my mind occupied. I opened my instant messenger program. I hadn't chatted with anyone in years as I looked through my friends' list. I noticed the same gal I messaged eight years prior is online. "WOW, she is still there," I'm thinking. I am still in awe of her picture and become nervous and excited. I messaged her again. She asks the same question: "Are you married?" I say, "Separated and Divorcing." We then start to chat. We chat about everything, how our parents are in New Mexico, we were both born in Denver, our taste in music, beer, you name it. It's like meeting the female version of ME.

We exchange phone numbers, and we call, and text each other. We spend hours and hours on the telephone just talking about any random thing in unison. She just had knee surgery from her job and is on workman's comp and must go from the Albuquerque area to El Paso, Texas, every week. I call her one day while she is en route to El Paso with her parents. I speak to her dad and mom by telephone, introducing ourselves to each other. I tell him I am a software engineer working in San Antonio, Texas, and I have started my own little company. Her dad says he is an electrical engineer, and we start talking about many things. It turns out the satellite antennas all of us Lost Boys used were tuned and created by this brilliant man who is now retired. Her mother is like my mom, loving, caring, collected, and steady-minded.

So, again we talked and talked forever. We just had to say hi to each other in a routine and see how the other was doing, or simply say, "You're on my mind." It got to the point her phone was about to die, and we couldn't do much talking because it was prepaid. I asked her to give me some information so I can add her to my cell phone plan, and we can talk and text unlimited. Once she had her new phone and number; we were inseparable via phone and text. I felt I was talking to someone who knew me inside and out without discussing our traumas and past.

It comes a time I need to meet her; I can't keep my mind from thinking of her. I fly her to San Antonio once she can walk. I still remember getting a bouquet of roses to greet her. The day is bright and perfect; even the air just seems as happy as I am. I wait in the gate area, waiting for her to walk out. She was in a light green summer dress, bright green eyes, and her make-up was perfect, her hair was radiant, I had to stare for a minute and say to myself, "Is that really her?" I guess we never discussed height differences because I am 5'4" and she's 5'9". I am so nervous and scared because I am significantly shorter than she is. She is known as "My love," and I am her "Shorty" later, she would learn that "El Chapo" means shorty as well, and I would be her Chapo at times. From that point forward. It was a biweekly trip on southwest airlines back and forth. We enjoyed each other a lot.

One night I had to get approval from her best friend. She calls her best friend up, and I am given the phone and provided a slew of questions. "What do you do? What interest do you have in my friend?" The next question she asked hit me with surprise, "You know about her past?" I said, "What do you mean?" She said, "Give the phone to her." Next thing you know, My Love is sitting down having to explain to me she has "Borderline Personality Disorder." I asked her if her friend's approval was vital to her. I explained that she needed to meet my sister. My sister was standoffish. I am 4 months into my separation, introducing her to My Love. They got along well, and after seeing the pictures of her, my sister could see how I fell for her as well. They talked, and she told her my dad would find it hard to get approval or acceptance.

I started to hear what it is like from her perspective and decided to google about the illness. I mean, I have PTSD and

Bipolar disorders. After reading all the symptoms, risk factors, and behavior. I can relate to some of them. My reaction triggered something so deep in her that she started crying. I felt so bad because she was on the kitchen floor, the same floor she was on her knees scrubbing because she wanted me to have a clean home. There are only two women in my life I have seen on their knees scrubbing the floor, my mom and My Love. She calmed down, and we started to talk. I began to take things in from a different perspective when it came to her and her disorder. I had to be very careful with what I said and how I responded. I had my own experiences, my own sensitivities and when it came to changing things in my realm for her. I told myself , "Ok, I can do that". My desire to make myself a better person was worth the motivation alone. I want to be a better man. The task at hand proved to be more difficult than I imagined. I love her, and she is not asking me to change myself into a better person. I want to do it myself. I spent the last 16 years yelling and name-calling. I don't want another 16 years of the same.

Having a small start-up company, I was all about business and making it work after a 16-year marriage ending in divorce. We got invited to a reception with the "Association of Old Crows" (AOC) San Antonio Chapter for St Patrick's day. The AOC is an organization for individuals who have common interests in Electronic Warfare (EW), Electromagnetic Spectrum Operations (EMSO), Cyber Electromagnetic Activities (CEMA), Information Operations (IO), and other information related capabilities[14]. The City of San Antonio had dyed the riverwalk green; people everywhere walked with green shirts, holding a green beer, and displaying their Irish heritage. My Love is Irish, and it only made things much more perfect. We went to the AOC dinner banquette, then went on

---

[14] 2021. *Association of Old Crows- Mission and History*. [online] Available at: <https://www.crows.org/page/missionandhistory>

a riverboat with bagpipe players piping. We invited a couple I knew professionally to be there with us on a double date. The husband was having a great time, drunk and yelling, "Pipers Pipe!" We had a blast!

It came time to go home, I asked her to put on her seatbelt, and it turned into a fiasco. She has lost a friend in High School to a seat belt in a deadly car accident, and it weighed heavy on her. I negotiated with her, and we agreed she needed to put it on or I would receive a ticket. We got home just talking about the events, and then we started to listen to music because we both loved it so much. I mean, we loved the same bands, Tool, Papa Roach, Linkin Park, Three Doors Down, Three Days Grace. I can keep naming a rock band, and we have heard them and named our favorite songs by each one.

Her favorite bands are Paparoach, Linkin Park, and Breaking Benjamin. Mine are Paparoach, Seether, Chevelle, and Tool. Everything we had was just a perfect dream. She had me watch a movie, The Notebook and she called our relationship her notebook kind of love, and I accepted it and liked it too.

It came time to meet her parents, I drove to the Albuquerque area of NM, and her dad gave me directions to the house. I met her dad. It was like I met myself in my older retirement years. I discovered he is a HAMM Radio operator, and I started talking to him and referring to things in Radio Q codes. I find out he has Parkinson's and myasthenia gravis, and the combination of both is scarce and brain debilitating diseases. We were both two nerds playing around with our words. The ladies would get something to make for dinner and let him and I spend time together. They decided it was time for me to meet her dad's best friend and wife—we met them at a small pizza joint. Dad's best friend started to ask me questions about myself. He stopped asking when I told him I was Military Intelligence (MI) in the Army. He began to talk about his son-in-law in a Special Mission Unit at the National Security Agency (NSA). I then asked him, "what is your son-in-law's name?" He said, "His name is. Mr. G. " I said, "I know him.", I asked him to call up Mr. G so I could talk to him. It had been a while since we had spoken to each other.

Here is a gist of that conversation:

Dad's Bestie: "Hey G, I have someone here who wants to talk to you."

Me:" Hey, Mr. G, this is someone from your past."

Mr. G: "Oh Shit, who is this?" (Laughing)

Me: "You bought me my first case of beer at Goodfellow. We were in Panama and Desert Storm together."

Mr. G: "Trivino, what the hell are you doing at my in-laws in New Mexico!"

I told him how I got there and how the link was her dad and his father-in-law. It made her dad happy to have someone his best friend likes as well, along with a military connection to his best friend's family. Her dad was happy. The next day, after sleeping on the couch, he and I sat down at the kitchen table as he ate his heated doughnut and bacon. He expressed how much he liked me, and I said we were alike. The Family Dynamic on her side is perfect!!

I took her to Espanola to meet mom on Mother's Day the following day. I told My Love that she needed to meet my mother. We met on neutral ground at my sister's house before taking her to meet dad. Well, mom turned out to be the hard one to please. Mom had all these intense questions. "What do you want with my son? Are you going to break his heart? Are you from a good family?" Mom just let questions fly. Mom said to me, "I don't know, Luis, you're not even divorced yet." We all just respected what mom said and kept our comments to ourselves. Next, we went to see dad. My mom asks dad if he wants to meet my girlfriend. Dad says, "Sure, mama." Man, those two hit it off like they had known each other forever. It turns out mom was the one who had her reservations, not dad. Those quickly changed when my mom noticed our devotion and love for each other. Something mom is all too familiar with in her own life, love and devotion.

We headed back to San Antonio, Texas, in two cars because we decided to move in together. We couldn't wait to start all new. We began to unpack and place her stuff in drawers, closets and mingle our stuff together. I worked from home, so we just hung out, watched TV while I worked on the couch. The day came when she would have to meet my kids. She quickly turned white as a ghost when I mentioned kids. She had this fear for some reason, and I tried to assure her it was ok. Well, one day, all three kids came over, they slept on the floor in front of the TV, and we had our bedroom. She had two little dogs, Abby and Harmony, they were both well-trained house dogs, and the kids just loved taking them out to potty. I'm saying to myself, wow, this is going to work! The middle kid has been my shadow since he was born and decided he wanted to sit in between us on the couch. It turns out he just wanted to be close to both of us. But it was tough to convince "the disorder" that's what it was. From her perspective my son wanted to keep us apart and the disorder preyed on that fear. My Love loves the kids; she loves all kids; it's the disorder that has its issue. We worked it all out, and things were getting normal again. I spoke to her mom, and she suggested I read some books if I am serious about her daughter. I decided to read some books on the disorder. We went to Barnes and Noble, and I bought my first book "Stop Walking on Eggshells" by Randi Kreger[15]. The disorder did not like me

---

[15] *Mason, Paul T. Kreger, Randi Stop Walking on Eggshells. Oakland, CA :New Harbinger : Distributed by Publishers Group West, 1998.b*

reading that book; the disorder wanted to deny anything wrong with itself. One evening I found the disorder while talking to an old boyfriend, and I chastised her for it, and she didn't like it. The disorder and I disagreed, and the disorder got so mad and it moved in with some friends.

My Love was sorry, but the disorder just made a poor decision, so I blame the disorder, not my wife. There is a big difference. My wife is faithful, and sometimes the disorder clouds her mind when she is most vulnerable. I mean, my wife is perfect, but it's the disorder that gets in the way. So, I read more and used some tools so we can work together at it. We are working on it, and it is going super well. We went to a tattoo shop because she wanted to cover up a tattoo and start a new memory from something bad. We eventually met the coolest tattooist. He is much like me, and she likes him too. We began to hang out, eat at different places. We go to Barnes and Noble and hang out.

Trivino/ A Notebook of Love-My Story on Mental Health

There is a funny story where they both were kicked out because he was talking to a loud marine from his high school days. This guy is saying out loud, "He is a badass mothering marine chasing skirts!" I go outside, and they are laughing. I'm like, "What happened?", they both said, "We got kicked out of Barnes and Noble. Because the people thought we were rude." It was just best friends all around. I like Karaoke, and he likes Karaoke, so we went to some of our favorite places to sing. We regularly attend a small dive bar together, and it is where we have our karaoke family. Everyone knows each other, and we all love each other like family. When someone needed to move, we all pitched in on the day of the move.

We spend a lot of time with our friends. Mainly with two couples, the men both own and operate tattoo shops separately. We are always going out to eat dinner, drink beer and sing Karaoke. They were all part of our karaoke and tattoo club.

My wife would get a lot of tattoos because we love them and sometimes must agree where she wanted to get them. Because the disorder's behavior would have her face covered with tattoos and without thinking about some things sometimes. It came to the point when My Love needed to work, so she got a job at a local fancy restaurant as a server, and she loved it. It was what she is used to, and she introduced me to a whole new world of workers. Cooks, servers, managers, she had me watch the movie "Waiting"; I learned a lot of things about the food industry that is so hard on the workforce. The wait staff average hourly rate is 2 dollars an hour. If the cooks mess up on orders, it affects the servers' tips. If there is a bartender, the bar tips are shared with all the bar staff. I became friends with them all. I would go in with my professional look, and they would treat me like I was family, and I enjoyed being around them.

I would regularly ask her to marry me, and she would say no. I tried twice already. I said, "Come on," she would not budge till one day I called her dad and asked him what he thought if I asked for her hand in marriage. He said he would love to have me as his son-in-law. I asked My Love in the parking lot of Barnes and Noble. She said, "No." I said, "I spoke to your dad and asked his permission." She said, "What did he say?" I told her what he said, she then responded with "Yes!" We went straight to the ring store; she called her dad, she told him what happened, and we are now buying a ring. We had a bachelor/bachelorette party with her work family and our karaoke family combined. We had an open bar tab for everyone, and we had a blast. We obtained our marriage license and then got married by the justice of the peace.

We one day discover her dad's diseases are taking a turn for the worse. My wife is heart-stricken. We find out my dad is not doing too well either. He is in the hospital. We decided to move to NM to be closer to family. We stayed with my parents in the adobe house for about a month. She loved staying up with dad and soon discovered dad just wanted to have attention and conversation with his kids. We kids avoided him and his outrageous comments and his stories about war and violence. My wife showed me my way back to my dad. I started to spend Thursday evenings with dad to watch a movie. Little did I know not correctly arranging this separation with her disorder would cause issues. My Love loved that I spent time with dad and I started healing from years of abuse. Behind the scenes, the disorder tells her, "He is leaving." Her fear sets in as I walk out the door to spend a movie night with my dad.

Meanwhile, we went to see her dad, and he was getting worse and worse. I noticed subtle changes in her behavior, and she was sleeping more. It turns out the disorder was going into a downward spiral, and it triggered the "Fight or Flight" mechanism, and she went away. Some guy in another city promised the disorder to the world and more. I notified her mom. My god, her mom, is the GREATEST. She already knew how to handle this. I mean, I wish I had her intuition and judgment regarding the disorder. But I guess that comes with mom's intuition. Her comments were, "I was afraid this was going to happen." My mother-in-law loves my wife with a mother's love like my own mother and perhaps a degree more. But mom also hates the behavior of the disorder.

I spoke with mom about it. She reminded me I knew what I was getting myself into, and I agreed and knew this could happen. I just never noticed the triggers at all. It triggered my PTSD. I started losing sleep at night. I went back to San Antonio after my dad got better. I followed Mom's advice saying she may be back, but I had to move on and take care of myself. The idea that this happens as a defense mechanism made me think. The disorder always runs in a "Fight or Flight" situation. I never flee. I chose to fight in a "Fight or Flight" situation, but the disorder always takes a flight, as far away as someone will rescue it. I was like, "What the Fuck!" She quickly reminded me it is the disorder's behavior doing this. My Love may be back, and we will need to deal with the pieces. I decided to move back to San Antonio, and the tattooist helped me move into my apartment. I tried to explain to him it's the disorder's behavior that it is not My Love doing that. They are together in her head, and they have a union that borders reality and psychosis. She winds up back at mom's house, and MOM, just super mom like mine, knows what to do. She brings back my wife, not to me but to the reality of how things are.

We decide to move back in together as roommates, my wife's shame affects her, but the disorder doesn't care. I told my wife I loved her, and I forgive her. We started to communicate well, and we began to open up to each other, and we finally figured it out. Our groove of communication and acceptance is incredible. I accepted my wife and her disorder as our love is unconditional. During this time, I learned not to yell, control my anger, and speak more effectively with my wife. These changes make any person better, not just a man. I made these positive changes in my behavior quickly because I love my wife, which I want to make for me. We became the best of friends beating the odds in recovering from the incident prior. I tell her I love her unconditionally and genuinely mean it today.

We communicated, she needed limits on things we set and agreed on them together. We love concerts so much we went to many in San Antonio, like the River City Rockfest, Oyster Bake, you name it, we were there. We wound up raising a foster daughter from one of her ex-husbands, we provided the stability she needs to graduate from high school. I worked as a consultant in the IT industry after getting rid of the company and barely broke even. We discovered she was getting a massive headache. Turns out she needed a VP shunt, a small plastic tube that helps drain extra cerebrospinal fluid from the brain. She had two revisions, and one procedure turned septic. We never swayed. We stayed loyal and true, leaning on each other the whole time; we were inseparable.

   The time came when we had to move back to New Mexico to be closer to our widowed mothers. We first stopped at mom's adobe house; we picked up Chester, a Pitbull dog, the best therapy for her. He senses when she needs help, and he responds to her, keeping the disorder at bay. Her disorder is always nervous and looking for an escape. We bought some land by my sister's place; we moved into my sister's place because no one has been there in years since dad passed away. We have been in this married bliss for many

years. We had gone through so much
together that we resemble a couple who
seriously has their shit together. We have
the stability most couples wish they had, in
love, finances, and communication. My wife
prides herself as a loving, loyal wife. I have
the security code to unlock her phone; she
has the code to mine. We have nothing to
hide. Most of all, mom is proud of how we
became a married couple. I went through a
few stressful job transitions, I finally got a
job that paid us a significant amount of
money, and we started to save and build a
401k. She built her credit with me as well.
We are making plans to grow and die old
together. I want to build on the property so
the house can have equity and help her
survive if I pass away before she does. I love
my wife and want to make sure she is taken
care of if I pass before she does. The
disorder wants to move into a
manufactured home right away. So, we all
agreed to wait and see what happens once
we save enough to make a more dedicated
decision.

Trivino/ A Notebook of Love-My Story on Mental Health

Life is great! We have taken our mothers to Las Vegas, and they both disappear from us. We are concerned about where they are at 2 a.m. in the morning. They decide to sneak out; my mom has a drink in her hand while her mom is pushing my mom in her chair everywhere, lol. They are just like two kids and curious about a new world. We are going to NYC for an anniversary. We went to the National Mall because I wanted to surprise her and show her the Ruby Red slippers from the Wizard of Oz, her favorite movie of all time. We meet Papa Roach, Breaking Benjamin, and we get front-row seats almost everywhere we go. We are doing this together.

Then my younger brother's disorder started to interfere with her triggers. I am constantly asking him not to come around drinking or act irritated; it scares my wife. I made stances for her mental health, and I needed to keep the monsters away from my wife. My little brother and his friends terrify the disorder, so I prioritize my wife's mental health and stress level. My cousin from Gallup moves in with us, and we all establish a relationship with him; and my wife and I love this cousin. We have a ton of laughs, watching our TV shows together, playing a specific movie to go to bed to, going to places, road trips, and just living life.

COVID 19 hits, and we are in lockdown now. I do all the shopping, and my wife has no idea how bad the virus can be and how much of a killer it is. I express my concerns about her hand cleaning procedures, and the disorder does not like that. My wife inside knows I mean the best, but the disorder clouds her mind with what is safe and unsafe with this deadly virus stopping the world in its tracks. While COVID started, my mom started to go in and out of the hospital. She is starting to deteriorate from the long-term side effects of the drugs used to avoid her kidney rejection. It places a lot of stress on everyone, my little brother included. On

Trivino/ A Notebook of Love-My Story on Mental Health

July 2nd, 2020, my mom passed away in her house on hospice. My sister, wife, and her mom are together in my mother's room in her last moments. We can't believe it; my mom is gone. Ironically only women smelled incense and roses at mom's moment of death. My mom prayed with her rosary every day. It gave me faith and assisted my grieving with the loss of my mama. I am a true mama's boy and needed something to help me.

My sister always wanted a manufactured home on her property, and my wife loves the idea of living in mom's house and fixing it up. My wife told my sister she would love to move into mom's house and take it off her hands. The disorder was scared to say something to me because it decided without thinking first. It took her 3 months to tell me what she decided and I totally agree with my wife's decision. My sister and her husband had been taking care of our parents for the past 15 years and never made themselves a priority. In my mind they earned the right to move and live where and how they want without being forced into mom's home. My love and I made a great team. Mom and dad financed the house on a reverse mortgage, and it is an ongoing tug of war to purchase the house right now. We have been trying for over a year, and the disorder wants changes done to make things comfortable. I haven't been around a lot because I must get firewood, and I have been working on pottery and helping friends just trying to keep myself busy.

My wife decided she would like to get some Dialectical Behavior Therapy (DBT) because she doesn't like the disorder and its behavior. I support my wife in all that she does. I just had no idea I wasn't validating her and her needs to better communicate. She finds a therapist who takes our insurance. She started her therapy and set some goals; it takes a year to graduate from, and she did it independently. The sessions are for her.

Then some new issues start to arise; she will face her trauma therapy and confide in me she doesn't want to do it. I supported her and encouraged her to tell her therapist not to continue trauma therapy. I guess the disorder stops her from speaking and being openly honest about the deep and dark things. So she holds everything deep inside where it is festering and growing all while holding a smile for all to see. My wife says she is in a funk, and it may take a while to get out of it. I tell her we will make it together lovingly, and I will be by her side no matter what. I need to know what she needs from me. Meanwhile, she is in a deep internal struggle with the disorder and herself, using the tools given to her in therapy. We all notice and try to talk to my wife; the disorder lurks in the shadows listening to everything we say, and it has a big hold on her using her fears against her. Man, this DBT stuff is taking a massive toll on her self-image. My wife used to be happy. My wife is more sensitive to words thanks to the disorder's way of thinking. It is hard to get a definite answer. I wish I could participate; I want to understand what I need to do and learn to work this through as a couple. Why won't my wife talk to me anymore? I keep reminding myself this is her battle, she must do it, but the disorder is always there. The disorder uses her emotions and fear, tempting her to run. Things are getting difficult for the disorder to communicate. Her provider decided to change her meds and almost wean her off her anti-anxiety medications. GREAT! Another fucking challenge. All this comes at a huge cost to her and our relationship, we are arguing about anything and everything. Why am I always the bad guy when negotiating with the disorder? We used to be a team. What happened?

My sister, her husband, my wife, and I decided to go to Las Vegas for Thanksgiving. I'm a little tipsy, and the disorder does not want me around. We have been tipsy many times and happy in social settings. "What is different this time?" I ask myself. I ask my wife why we feel like we are roommates and not best friends anymore. My wife couldn't answer while she was holding everything inside and was hiding in the shadows. The disorder is cornered with the question and doesn't answer. The disorder just keeps hiding; I say some words I wish I could take back because I promised never to say them. I say, "I think I may have given up on us. Please help me understand," followed by a few more things, and in an instant, my wife blinks her eyes. Her facial features change as if a record is being reset, opens her eyes. I see a different person, the color of her eyes changes and there is a dark glare. I saw the disorder face to face, for the first time. It is as if a totally different person or personality has just emerged from her, and this person is NOT my wife. Someone must almost experience this to know what I am describing.

My wife and I decide it is best to go home a day early, and my spiral of shock and PTSD triggers are setting in. I'm trying to resolve it. I'm trying to cope; I'm trying to adjust to comments like, "I've been wanting to divorce for a year, but I didn't want to take responsibility." I mean, this disorder has caused my wife to become confused, illogical, and delusional all together.

Her mom is used to noticing the disorder and its dissociations and personality splits, and this one hits her by surprise. The next thing I know, the therapist is encouraging her to leave. What? The therapist believes she can make it on her own. Does the therapist see the disorder? I mean, the therapist thinks she knows my wife. WOW! The whole family is in shock. I decided to support my wife in her transition. Thinking it is part of her DBT, I let the disorder know I propose a peace accord. My wife can take all the time she needs to get through this; she doesn't need a relationship to complicate things if she wants to move forward with her therapy. I propose we remain abstinent until this is over. The disorder says, "I'm afraid I can't do that. I am speaking to a 38-year-old staff sergeant in Afghanistan, and he is coming in on January 12th to pick up his daughter and retire in Ohio." I'm in shock we haven't had soldiers in Afghanistan since the end of August 2021. I received new intel. I must adjust my planning, just as I was taught and trained in the army. Could the disorder have been catfished, or is it lies and manipulation to get away and reset and reground herself? But the disorder denies it. No one knows if he is for real. In the meantime, I see suspicious activity in our bank account. I notify the banks; I am forced to report this to my government employer. I turned off her cell phone, but she wired 200 bucks for support somewhere. I am arguing with the disorder, who feels I am taking everything away from my wife to continue this behavior. Meanwhile, my wife is inside somewhere lost, confused, and perhaps the most terrified ever. If it is not a catfish, what kind of man would do this to someone in a sensitive state?

We have changed our Facebook status to separate, and it has triggered surprise and shock in everyone because they all know my wife and I were good and solid. But the disorder crept up on us like a stealthy ninja assassin. Before this happened, she and I were talking a while back, and she explained to me how she has this relationship with the disorder. She said, "if I ever want to run, keep me here. I don't want to go; I want to break the cycle." I can describe it as that moment of clarity an alcoholic has before deciding to stop drinking. Supermom and I are trying hard to break the cycle, but the disorder has an excellent grasp on my wife denying me. Mom has seen this before and is scared we all may have to move on. Right now, I sit wondering if the disorder will erase me. I may lose my wife to something I cannot touch and only see in her eyes.

Trivino/ A Notebook of Love-My Story on Mental Health

To my notebook love:

Hi, My Love! I hope you are doing well. My sister, your best friend, came up to me today, stating you were asking her if I loved you. More so, how could I love you with all this baggage and trauma you carry everyday? My love for you is so complex that it is hard to answer, alone, with words and gestures. I felt you needed to know who I really am and how my journey has brought us here. Which is why I am writing this notebook of my story on mental health, followed with this little note to explain everything to you. I, too, am like you, broken and in pieces. I truly understand your battle within your head and the emotions that run amuck. You know all my complexities, inefficiencies, faults, qualities, and best traits. I am an open book to you, and as a result, I wrote one. I am the one who should ask if I am worthy of your love. I should ask why you love me? I know many things I have said and done are tearing at you internally, and for that, I am eternally sorry. I am sorry you are going through that alone. I, too, am "Broken" in your terms and all too familiar with your inner struggles. I know well enough that I accept your mind, body, soul, and all the inner selves of you. I still and will always and forever love you. As husband and wife, best friends, broken soul to a broken soul, my demons to your demons, my Love for you is UNCONDITIONAL. If I am unworthy of Love, and you feel the same, then we are made for each other. If our notebook saves one life, then that is even a more extraordinary gift our Love has to offer. You are more than worthy of Love.

Love Shorty

Chapter Seven

Becoming a Man

"The secret of change is to focus all of your energy not on the fighting the old, but on building the new." - **Socrates**

Uncertainty

I have just handed my wife the notebook and signed the letter. I have no idea what to expect, how she will react. At least I got to show her she is worthy of love, and I do love her. Everyone is worthy of love regardless of their past. Those who feel unworthy are the ones who need love the most.

In the meantime, I have my own journey that I am taking to be my own man. So, like Socrates states above, I am starting to focus my energy on the new me. Will she come back? I don't know, I can't worry about that right now; she is in her own battle, and I can't be there to hold her this time. I listened to the country song "The Man I Want to Be" by Chris Young for the first time. It made my eyes flow a river of tears, as the saying goes. A song that keeps defining my world of change from my beginning till now. While separated and struggling to understand what happened, I am working hard to be the man I want to be.

I broke the cycle of violence I inherited from my dad and refused to pass it on. For me, that is the greatest gift to pass on in the generations of Trivino's to come. I have attended a few counseling sessions at the Indian Health Services, and I love every minute of it. My first session showed me I have more work ahead of me, and I'm doing this for me, and it will prepare me for the uncertainty that I face. My first cognitive-behavioral therapy (CBT) session got my attention, and I want to apply what I learned. In the meantime, I am trying to deprogram the programs in my head from "Shoot! Move! Communicate!" to something like "Listen, Patience, Communicate." and it's hard.

Men, we can do this. We need to stop being stubborn old men and become new men! Being the oldest and the rock in our marriage I seldom talk to someone when I must try and resolve issues within the family circle. I discovered talking to my therapist has been most productive in my mental stability and aids my understanding and communicating with my wife while she goes through her process of mental re-grounding. I encourage any man who is the rock in a family to just find a therapist to talk to at least once a quarter. It does you some good and provides better tools in dealing with family issues and decision-making skills.

Mental Health Illness is All Around Us! For some unknown reason we all tend to dismiss it or downplay it by choosing labels, he is "Homeless", he is an "Addict", he just needs some help.

The following statistical show illustrates 1 in every 5 adults suffers from any mental illness.

• 21% of U.S. adults experienced mental illness in 2020 (52.9 million people). This represents 1 in 5 adults.

• 5.6% of U.S. adults experienced serious mental illness in 2020 (14.2 million people). This represents 1 in 20 adults.

• 16.5% of U.S. youth aged 6-17 experienced a mental health disorder in 2016 (7.7 million people)

• 6.7% of U.S. adults experienced a co-occurring substance use disorder and mental illness in 2020 (17 million people)

If you grew up in a household of 5, chances are at least one family member has a mental illness.

Much worse, if you are raising a family of 5, the chances are the same. The statistics above infer the one who may be afflicted is an adult, and could it be you? Men, mental health is our responsibility and one we should take seriously as beer on Friday night after work. It is a responsibility we owe to those we love.

Suicide Awareness

According to the Mayo Clinic, "Suicidal thoughts have many causes. Most often, suicidal thoughts are the result of feeling like you can't cope when you're faced with what seems to be an overwhelming life situation. If you don't have hope for the future, you may mistakenly think suicide is a solution. You may experience a sort of tunnel vision, wherein in the middle of a crisis you believe suicide is the only way out." Suicide is a major health problem, and the global suicide mortality rate amounts to 1.4% of all deaths worldwide. Most suicides are related to psychiatric disease, with depression, substance use disorders, and psychosis as the most relevant risk factors. About 20 veterans commit suicide a day, and nearly three-quarters are not under VA care. My story includes two stories of suicide where mental health was a factor, and one was a veteran. We have all seen the happy faces of suicide days before the tragic loss happens. Let us become more aware and learn how to manage the tip-off of a suicidal person to the individuals capable of helping them through their duress.

Words as Weapons

Abuse comes in many forms, and we can inflict that just by being a manly man. We come home from a long day at work, tired, frustrated, and the questions from the family come, and we snap. Are we the problem? According to an article in Psychology Today, "verbal aggression produced larger effects than familial, physical abuse. There's evidence too that exposure to verbal abuse in childhood actually alters the structure of the brain." I'm not saying to change you but to change the pattern or situation. My wife and I had a great tool. She gave me 30 minutes at home to destress from work. I could vent, play a game, anything I wanted to do. After 30 minutes, she could ask me anything, and we were okay. My wife has a favorite song, "Words as Weapons," by Seether, and its title is vital as a topic. Weapons do one thing; they destroy and kill. As a veteran trained in weapons and tactics, it is very easy to use word vomit to react and attack. It's how we are trained to survive.   We must give words the same respect as a gun, they both kill, and the damage lasts forever. Words used as weapons leave deep scars that NEVER heal. I may have learned this lesson too late, and I take responsibility for that.

Do Something

I realized I should have been more involved in therapy with my wife from my mistakes in the past few months. I was not in the same session with her, because this is her journey. But willing to learn more of what she needs from me to be a better man and provide a happier marriage. Support speaks louder with action than listening and giving advice or critiques. Fifteen years we did things according to what worked for us, but that changed, and I failed to recognize it. Complacency in a marriage can become a threat if too many minor issues go unresolved. Because we had such a great groove and things were usually working, I failed to remember she has a disorder despite working well together.

Remove the Stigma

Society needs to remove the stigma of shame associated with AMI. The illness is responsible for the behavior, and don't judge the person or family. The families struggle to piece together the broken fragments caused by the behaviors and actions of a loved one with AMI. There should be no shame in saying Luis had a mental breakdown, and he is seeking the help he needs. The responsibility is twofold for those who served. I am sure your military story is like mine. Remember, the illness can be genetically linked, and there is no way anyone can change that. So, why punish the patient or family with shame. I knew the possibilities of the disorder's behavior in my wife, and I accepted them when I fell in love with her. It is who she is, and resolving the issue is possible; there is no shame in that.

Get Involved

The laws need to change and include input and concerns from the patient's family unit or support unit when a person is in mental distress. Lives will be saved when the doctors and physicians have the tools to help. Right now, the privacy laws force the criminalization of mental health patients; there needs to be a symbiotic relationship between a patient's Dr and the family unit. Mental illness is not a crime, and we shouldn't treat individuals as such. Make the issues of mental illness awareness a topic where it's permitted and spread a message of understanding and compassion.

Meanwhile

So, for now, I am trying to do me. I plan to purchase this old house and hold to some promises I made. I am like this old house. We both have great potential for improvement and good modifications. If that also means fixing us. I am already getting the tools I need to be a better man; they serve me a more significant purpose if they help me show more love and support for my wife. What harm is there to that? My dad assisted me into becoming a man in a harsh world, and he made me a tough motherfucker. My self-improvements define me. I am a man, my man. I am becoming the better man I want to be.

Dad, I love and forgive you.

☐

Need Immediate Help in An Emergency?

If you or a loved one is in immediate danger <u>calling 911 and talking with police</u> may be necessary. It is important to notify the operator that it is a psychiatric emergency and ask for police officers trained in <u>crisis intervention</u> or trained to assist people experiencing a psychiatric emergency.

Need Immediate Help in A Crisis?

<u>National Suicide Prevention Lifeline</u> – Call 800-273-TALK (8255) If you or someone you know is in crisis—whether they are considering suicide or not—please call the toll-free Lifeline at 800-273-TALK (8255) to speak with a trained crisis counselor 24/7.

The <u>National Suicide Prevention Lifeline</u> connects you with a crisis center in the Lifeline network closest to your location. Your call will be answered by a trained crisis worker who will listen empathetically and without judgment. The crisis worker will work to ensure that you feel safe and help identify options and information about mental health services in your area. Your call is confidential and free.

<u>Crisis Text Line</u> – Text NAMI to 741-741 Connect with a trained crisis counselor to receive free, 24/7 crisis support via text message

<u>National Domestic Violence Hotline</u> – Call 800-799-SAFE (7233) Trained expert advocates are available 24/7 to provide confidential support to anyone experiencing domestic violence or seeking resources and information. Help is available in Spanish and

other languages.

<u>National Sexual Assault Hotline</u> – Call 800-656-HOPE (4673)

Connect with a trained staff member from a sexual assault service provider in your area that offers access to a range of free services. Crisis chat support is available at <u>Online Hotline</u>. Free help, 24/7.

If you would like to have your organization and information added to the list, please email me at luis@mynotebook.love

Made in the USA
Middletown, DE
06 April 2023